30 DAYS TOWARD HEALING YOUR GRIEF

A WORKBOOK FOR HEALING

T0275177

Danielle DuBois Morris
and Kristen N. Alday

Church Publishing
NEW YORK

Church Publishing
19 East 34th Street
New York, NY 10016
www.churchpublishing.org

Cover design by Jennifer Kopec, 2Pug Design
Interior design and layout by Beth Oberholtzer Design

Library of Congress Cataloging-in-Publication Data
A record of this book is available from the Library of Congress.

ISBN-13: 978-0-8192-3327-1 (pbk.)
ISBN-13: 978-0-8192-3328-8 (ebook)

Printed in the United States of America

Contents

Introduction

Congratulations!

In the first line of his book *A Grief Observed*, C. S. Lewis wrote, "No one ever told me that grief felt so like fear."* Let's face it, grief can not only seem overwhelming but indeed, often terrifying. That's why coming face to face with grief takes great courage. So, congratulations. By picking up this book you have had your first victory over grief; you have made the decision to face it, walk through it, and to turn your grief into meaningful living.

What is different about this book?

Grieving is a private club that no one really wants to join. Those who have not experienced the pain of grief can never fully understand the complexity of emotions, physical symptoms, and mental anguish that affects the person who mourns. Both the Rev. Danielle Morris and the Rev. Kristi Alday first experienced the pain of grief when they suffered the deaths of their fathers when they were but teenagers. Sadly, both have had many other members of their family die over the years. They are members of the club and want to reach out to others who are grieving. This book is the result of their research and their personal experience of nearly twenty years of facilitating grief support groups.

30 Days toward Healing Your Grief is a workbook that is written to invite you into a virtual grief support group. The stories that you will read are from real people who have gone through real grief. To protect confidentiality, the names have been changed and the stories are, in actuality, compilations of several stories told by those who share your pain. While each person's grief is unique, and no two people grieve the same

---

* C. S. Lewis, *A Grief Observed* (New York: Harper & Row, 1961), 1.

way, chances are you will find that many of their stories are your story. Their pain is your pain. Most importantly, their victories will lead you toward victories of your own. The questions asked in this workbook are similar to those asked during grief support groups and help you move from "they died" to "they lived" and, finally, to "I should live to honor our relationship." As you find the courage to answer the questions in the workbook, you will begin to write your own brave, survival story.

While the sadness and your painful memories of your loved one will never completely leave you, the consuming sorrow you feel today will begin to heal through the abundant Grace of our Lord. And so we continue our daily prayers for your healing in the knowledge that our compassionate Lord, who loves you more than you can possibly imagine, sends you his peace.

What Am I Supposed to Do with the Pain?

For I, the Lord your God, hold your right hand;
it is I who say to you, "Do not fear, I will help you."
—ISAIAH 41:13

"You know the worst part about grief? When the funeral is over, people stop coming by, the food's gone, and that's when grief hits," says Nancy, a woman facing the recent death of her beloved grandmother. "And there you are, all alone with this horrible ache in your heart. What are you supposed to do with the pain?"

"Eat the casseroles," says Ray, a man whose wife had died. "Eat them alone, at the table where you once ate dinner with your wife. Alone. That's the key word. Alone."

Grief is indeed a lonely job. Bereavement can be filled not only with unquenched sorrow, but with confusion, anger, remorse, and guilt all rolled up into a vast array of mixed emotions. Sometimes you wonder if you're losing your mind. What are you supposed to do with the pain?

When one man received the news that his friend was dying and wanted to see him one last time, the man's heart told him to leave work and go to him immediately. The man wanted to tell his friend how much he appreciated his friendship, how much he loved him, how much he would miss his companionship.

Yet, like so many men balancing the demands of a hectic family life and a successful though exhausting career, he was torn between his responsibilities and his emotions. Each day he would plan to visit his friend, but each day there would be one last detail holding him back. By the time he was able to free his schedule and go to his friend, it was too late. His dear friend had died before the man could get there. Sorrow enveloped him, paralyzing his very thoughts like a powerful hand crushing down on him; catching his breath in its grasp, the force of grief enveloped him. And so, Jesus wept.

Simon had been married for over forty years. "I didn't even know how to turn on the oven when Margaret died. My wife did all the cooking. And the washing machine? I had no idea it was so complicated. Not only do I feel alone, but helpless."

Our Lord also suffered the anguish of grief. He shares our sorrow and longs to comfort us. As you go through your day, try to imagine Jesus standing next to you as you read and pray. He will be there. Take hold of his hand. Listen for his voice. Feel his presence.

1. Has there been a time in your grief when you felt completely engulfed by your pain? When you have felt your grief would never end?

_____

_____

_____

_____

_____

_____

"I will never get over this," says Marnie. "Our house caught on fire. We still don't know what caused it, but one of our children didn't make it out. My husband kept going into the house, but the flames were too much. He couldn't get Ronnie out. When I think, was he afraid? Did he call out for me? I am just haunted by that. I don't know that I can stand the pain either. I'm never going to get over this."

Sara had not shared much during the first meeting of her grief group. At the beginning of the second meeting she blurted out "What am I supposed to do with this endless, mind-numbing, aching pain?" Her eyes flashed wildly as she caught her breath. "I can't sleep, my body hurts, and my mind is chaos," she continued. Adding with a shaking voice she said, "My throat hurts and I am always sick at my stomach. And the worst part is sometimes I think I see Chloe on a crowded sidewalk. I try to speed up to catch her, my heart racing and my palms sweating. Then the pain jabs me with a fresh punch as I remember the accident."

Chloe was Sara's older sister and they had always been very close. On an early evening in December Chloe and her boyfriend George had gone for a drive to look at Christmas lights around town. The weather had been bad but now everything looked fluffy and white like a village in a snow globe. The police believe that the left turn arrow on the stop signal had appeared and George and Chloe moved into the intersection. At the same time, a car driving way too fast in the other lane skidded on a slick spot. It began to spin out of control. Five cars were involved in the accident, including the car that George and Chloe were in.

As Sara wept and trembled, she continued, "My beautiful sister was decapitated. I keep seeing that beautiful face. Oh my God," she cried out, "I can't take this!"

2. What is the worst time of day for you? When does your pain seem most intense?

_____

_____

_____

_____

_____

_____

"Sundays are the worst," says Jillian. "You go to church and see everyone with their families and you are alone. By yourself. The seat next to me feels so empty. My husband was only thirty-two when he died. I'm only thirty. People think because I'm young, I'm okay. But I'm not. And people in the church don't talk to me the way they used to when we were a couple."

"And there is no one to go to lunch with after church. Sure, people invite you but it's awkward. They don't know what to say or how to say it. So I go home and eat another casserole from the freezer. When those run out, I have no idea what I'm going to do," laughs Nancy.

"I can relate to that," says Ginger. "I kept telling my grandmother that I would go and see her and we'd go to lunch. I always have a hectic schedule at work and just kept putting it off. Now, if I go out to lunch, that's when I feel the worst."

3. Has there been a time recently when, in your grief, you felt the presence of God?

_____

_____

_____

_____

_____

_____

"I think God sent me a rose. I know it sounds silly, but right outside my dad's kitchen was his favorite rose bush. It was early spring; there was still some snow on the ground, way too early for roses to bloom. I went over to his house to start packing up his stuff and went out to the trash. I was feeling very guilty about throwing out some of his things. Coming back into the house, I noticed there was a bloom on one of the bushes. A big ole bloom. That made me smile. It was as if my dad and God were telling me it was okay."

4. When you feel as if you could use the presence of God, what might you do to draw him near?

_____

_____

_____

_____

_____

_____

"I got really mad at my friend Bree," Amy said. "We were having coffee and I was sharing with her my pain because obviously God had turned away from me. Bree only listened for a few minutes before she looked up and said, 'Amy, God does not turn away from us, we turn away from him.'"

Amy paused for a moment, frowning when she continued, "I was so angry with Bree. I thought she was my friend. Was she saying that this pain was my fault?" As her story unfolded Amy described an experience sitting in the park by a fountain. "I was just staring at the water. Staring, staring. Everything seemed still and I remembered what Bree had said."

After what seemed like a long time, she put her head down and said, "Please don't think I am crazy but I looked at that fountain and I asked Jesus if he was really living water, would he please ease my pain. I stood up and went and put my hand in the water. And then I felt a tingling all over my body." She continued, "It was if the water said, 'All you had to do was ask. I am always with you.'"

 Healing prayer for today: Hold my hand, Lord. I cannot go through this without you.

Does God Care?

Are not two sparrows sold for a penny? Yet not one of them will fall to the ground unperceived by your Father. And even the hairs of your head are all counted. So do not be afraid; you are of more value than many sparrows.
   —Matthew 10:29–31

"Sometimes just getting out of bed in the morning takes all the energy I have," says Grace, a recent widow. "When I finally get out of bed and I think about facing a day without my husband, all I want to do is crawl back under the covers. It's been three months and I still cry all the time. I pray very hard, asking God to help me, but I'm not making any progress. I'm beginning to wonder, does God care?"

A foretaste of God's love for us is revealed in the love we have for each other. When the person we love dies, the emptiness left behind causes great sorrow. We cry out to God in our grief, and it's not unusual to wonder if he hears us.

Yet God does hear our pain and cares a great deal that we suffer. How can we know for sure? Because God concerns himself with the minute details of our lives, including the number of hairs on our heads. Even as Jesus was preparing for his own death, his thoughts were of us: "Do not let your hearts be troubled. Believe in God, believe also in me. In my Father's house there are many dwelling places. If it were not so, would I have told you that I go to prepare a place for you? And if I go and prepare a place for you, I will come again and will take you to myself, so that where I am, there you may be also" (John 14:1–3).

1. Did the death of your loved one cause you, even for a moment, to think that God didn't care that you were suffering? Explain how you felt that God was not present to you. Can you give it a word?

_____

_____

_____

_____

_____

_____

"Abandonment," says Margie. "I felt completely abandoned by God. My husband couldn't take watching our little boy Scotty die, so he left us. Here I was with huge hospital bills, getting evicted from our apartment because my ex-husband didn't pay the rent, no income because I lost my job staying in the hospital with Scotty, one child in the hospital, one with me day and night because I had no family to watch her and what was I going to do? Where the hell was God?"

"My word is unbearable," says Mike. "The grief of my father's death was unbearable. Then the family that I had always thought invincible, imploded. Everything I had thought of as 'truth' vanished. Friends did not know what to say to me so they avoided me. When I went to church it just made me sadder. I could not pray and really did not think it would do any good. Ultimately, I decided Jesus was a phony, just like all the other people and things I believed in were."

2. In what ways has God demonstrated his care for you?

_____

_____

_____

_____

_____

_____

"God came to my rescue through a nurse on the ward. She saw me washing my daughter in the ladies' room. She figured I was in trouble. I was embarrassed," said Margie. "But she said not to worry. All would be well. She prayed for me, but my heart was not in it. Later that day she sent a social worker to me and helped me with all sorts of things, including getting my daughter and me to a Ronald McDonald House, while she looked for a place for us to live. She was there when Scotty died. She held his hand and prayed for him to be received into heaven. I don't know what I would have done without her kindness. I know Jesus sent her to me."

3. How are you experiencing God's presence in your grief? Who has reached out God's loving arms to you? When you feel as if you could use the presence of God, what might you do to draw him near?

_____

_____

_____

_____

_____

_____

_____

"Prayer helps. I like saying the rosary," says Dale. "I can't get all the way through it, but it's okay. Yes, I cry. It's okay for men to cry, you know."

"I have a friend who always asks for me to walk with her every morning," says Gina. "I'm not an athlete, but one morning I said I'd go with her. I had been feeling so alone and I needed company. As we walked, it started to rain and then it stopped. And there was a rainbow. I know it sounds corny, but it reminded me of God's promise. And I wondered if my sweet Ethan could see rainbows in heaven. Were we sharing this moment? And it gave me great solace to think that we were."

 Healing prayer for today: Dear Lord, help me to know that you really care for me. Let me feel your presence.

DAY 3

Help Me, Lord!

In you, O Lord, I seek refuge; do not let me ever
be put to shame; in your righteousness deliver me.
Incline your ear to me; rescue me speedily. Be a rock
of refuge for me, a strong fortress to save me.
　　—PSALM 31:1–2

"I wake up in the morning praying that the death of our daughter was just a bad dream," says the mother of a five-year-old child who died of cancer. "I go into Stephanie's room, and see that she's not there and the reality that she's gone hits me all over again. Dear God, help me! I cannot bear this pain."

In Psalm 116:15 the psalmist writes, "Precious in the sight of the Lord is the death of his faithful ones." You, and your loved one who is now with God, are so very precious to your Lord. Jesus shares the pain you are enduring. Healing the pain of grief takes time. The good news is you don't have to go through the pain alone; your Lord waits for you to call upon his name. "I love those who love me; and those who seek me diligently will find me" (Proverbs 8:17). "Cast your burden on the Lord, and he will sustain you" (Psalm 55:22).

Will you ever get over your grief? Not completely, but the intense pain you are feeling now will begin to lessen. Coping with grief is like running a marathon. Sometimes you just have to keep going even though you have little strength. How? By remembering that God weeps with you, and since he cannot be defeated, neither can you.

1. Looking back at your grief, at what point did it feel as if you would never survive? What gave you the strength to carry on?

_____

_____

_____

_____

_____

_____

"Baby shampoo," says Grace. "Our baby only lived a few hours. I had the layette all set for our coming home. But she never came home. The layette collected dust but I just didn't have the heart to put it away. Then one day I ran out of shampoo. In desperation I got the shampoo from the layette. I washed my hair and cried that there was no baby's head to wash. I know this will sound weird, but all of a sudden I felt connected to her. I've been using baby shampoo ever since." Grace laughs, "And my hair is really shiny!"

2. When was a time when you felt defeated?

_____

_____

_____

_____

_____

_____

Scott shuffles in his seat, "The first time I tried to bake. What a mess! My wife was the cook, and I was the griller. I can whip up a barbeque, but a cake? It was my daughter's birthday and I wanted to bake the cake her mother always made for our kids. It came out so lopsided, and it was still kind of raw in the middle. I run a big company, but to do something as simple as bake a cake? I had to admit defeat."

3. It is not unusual to experience odd behavior that is truly unlike you but you can't seem to stop. Has that happened or is that happening to you?

_____

_____

_____

_____

_____

_____

"My two-year-old daughter climbed out of her crib at naptime. Somehow, she made it to our swimming pool and drowned. I can't bear the pain. It never leaves me. Sometimes I wake up coughing because I am dreaming I'm drowning with her. I hate when I see anyone else smile or seem happy. I have become a 'happiness assassin' because I feel they should feel at least a fraction of my pain. When I'm in the grocery store, dry cleaners, or anywhere for that matter, I carefully scope out my target. I call it a 'trifecta' if I can make three people in one store miserable. My husband is furious with me and is threatening to not let me leave the house alone. I can't do this Lord! Help me!"

4. Is there something that you're going through right now that feels out of control for you?

_____

_____

_____

_____

_____

_____

One couple is dealing with a relationship struggle that often accompanies the death of a child. "Tom wants sex all the time. That is the last thing on my mind," says Carolyn. "I just don't get it. He won't talk to me about Martha's death, but wants to have sex all the time. I want to talk about our daughter." Tom answers, "Sex takes my mind off of the fact that our daughter is dead. I need to feel life again. I need to be comforted. That's all. Talking about Martha brings the pain back. I don't want to deal with that."

Everyone grieves differently. For some sex becomes an outlet for pain. For others, sex, even with a loving spouse or significant other, is not something that is comforting. This couple realized that they were grieving differently. To save their marriage, Tom learned that talking about their daughter would lead Carolyn towards her healing. For Carolyn, Tom expressing his need for intimacy through sex, led the couple to an understanding that each needed something different from their relationship and from each other. They were grieving differently, but through understanding each other's pain, they could grieve together.

5. Do you find yourself doing anything differently today that you didn't do before the death of your loved one? Are you doing anything that might become harmful for you?

_____

_____

_____

_____

_____

"For me it was Valium," says Jenny. "My doctor gave me a couple of prescriptions, he said it would help my depression. I took them. Then when I went back for more he wouldn't give them to me. He referred me to a psychiatrist. Guess what? He gave me a prescription. My sister took them away from me. She was afraid I was taking too many. She said, 'You're out of control with these things. It's just numbing your pain!' Well, wasn't that the point? Yeah, I was numbing the pain. That's what I wanted to do. But when the pills were gone the pain was still there. I nearly became a drug addict! That's not me. I never took any pills before in my life. My sister was right. Thank goodness she took them from me."

 Healing prayer for today: Help me, Jesus!

Give Me Strength, Lord!

Your sun shall no more go down, or your moon
withdraw itself; for the Lord will be your everlasting
light, and your days of mourning shall be ended.
　—Isaiah 60:20

When it comes to grief, you have two choices. You can face it and walk through it, or be consumed by it. Making the decision to triumph over grief takes great courage. Yes, the battle will be painful, but it is a battle that's already been won for you. And you will come out the other side, victorious. How? By trusting in the power of your Lord to give you strength along the way.

"I didn't get to grieve my father," says Anna. "My stepmother insisted we show respect since he had been an Air Force officer. At the funeral, when the one plane left formation and took off toward heaven, I begin to cry. She pinched my leg to stop me. Not until my mother died, and a cousin gave me a photo of my dad, did I start to actually mourn him. It took thirty years but I am finally grieving him."

Henri J. M. Nouwen writes, "The first thing that Jesus promises is suffering: 'I tell you . . . you will be weeping and wailing . . . and you will be sorrowful.' But he calls these pains birth pains. And so, what seems a hindrance becomes a way; what seems an obstacle becomes a door; and what seems a misfit becomes a cornerstone. Jesus changes our history from a random series of sad incidents and accidents into a constant opportunity for a change of heart."**

One of the biggest myths about grief is that time will heal it. Time alone does not heal grief. A mourner must in fact walk through the Valley of the

---

** Henri J. M. Nouwen, *Out of Solitude: Three Meditations on the Christian Life*
(Notre Dame, IN: Ave Maria Press, 2004.), 55.

Shadow of Death. There is no bypass or shortcut. You can't go under, over, or around it. Additionally, if you begin the journey through the valley and you stop, turn around and go back, you will have to begin all over again. Grief must be worked through, even when it means to fully embrace the pain.

1. Are you willing to begin the journey through the valley? What motivated you to take the first step?

_____

_____

_____

_____

_____

_____

"I have to do this or I'm going to lose my mind," says Hillary. "I am frozen in time to when my mother died. I did everything for her towards the end. I was at her house every day. Now that she's gone, I'm lost. I can't keep going to her house every day and waiting for her to come back. One day I was sitting on her bed, smelling her pillow and noticed her scent was fading. That's when it hit me. She's not coming back and I have to accept that. As crazy as it sounds, I don't think I did until that moment."

2. How are you facing the pain head on?

_____

_____

_____

_____

_____

"I'm cleaning out my husband's closet. I know it's silly but with his clothes in the closet, it was like he wasn't totally gone. I kept a jacket of his. When the day gets too bad, I put on his jacket and it's like his arms are around me. I'm not ready to give up the jacket, but I'm making progress."

3. Are there times you feel isolated in pain? If so, how do you reach out for help? Who can you go to who will help you on your journey?

_____

_____

_____

_____

_____

_____

Margo reaches out through her phone. "I have this friend who has been so great. Leslie lets me call her and talk. She's a great listener. I tell her I need to talk, and to just put the phone down and let me rant, but she doesn't. She listens. What a powerful gift listening is!"

4. Sometimes when you grieve you may discover that you also grieve for someone else. Has there been someone in your past you have not grieved?

_____

_____

_____

_____

_____

_____

Sam says, "My twin sister died when I was six. At six you don't think anything much about grief. Sally was there one minute and gone the next. I worried a lot as a kid that I would die. When you are a child, all you think about is yourself. But recently a man in my office had a child die at the age of six, the same way my sister died. A drunk driver hit him as he was walking on the sidewalk. All these memories came flooding in. I was walking behind my sister when she got hit. I had blocked all that completely from my memory. Now I am grieving her."

 Healing prayer for today: Lord Jesus, help me to trust in you, give me strength to endure and heal me of my grief.

DAY 5

I Am in Complete Despair

Turn to me and be gracious to me, for I am lonely and afflicted. Relieve the troubles of my heart, and bring me out of my distress.
—Psalm 25:16–17

"What's the point of going on? Everything I did, I did for them," says a man whose wife and two children had been killed. "Now that they're gone, what's the point? I have nothing to live for."

Ever feel like you're drowning in sorrow? Have you had moments where you, too, have felt there is no point in going on with your life? You are not alone. We've all been there. While it may not seem worth the effort right now, be of good courage, for God has a joyful life planned for you. The widower in this story eventually re-married, had another child, and is looking forward to grandchildren. "I never thought I could be happy again. If you had told me that I could have a full life a second time, I wouldn't have believed you. But here I am, living proof that life can be good again."

Our Lord is a loving God. Jesus didn't just die on the cross for our sins; he rose again! He is a living God who can bring us out of the depths of despair. By trusting in his love, you will begin to find a new purpose for your life. Maybe not today, but soon.

1. Describe a time when you felt complete despair?

_____

_____

_____

_____

_____

"The day after the funeral," says Lydia. Her husband and son had been on a fishing trip. The boat capsized and their bodies had been lost at sea. "They never did find the body of my husband nor my son. We had a funeral, but with no bodies, so there was no closure. I keep fantasying that they are still alive somewhere. Then I wonder how they died. Was my son afraid? Did he call out for me? I feel not only despair, but utter helplessness."

"I understand that feeling of despair," says Craig. "We were sitting downstairs watching television when our daughter Margarete was upstairs taking a drug overdose. If I had gone into her room to check on her, maybe she'd be alive today. I didn't even know she was on drugs. I guess there were signs, but I didn't recognize them. Drug overdoses happen to other people's kids. I never dreamed it would happen in our family. Why didn't we know? Every time I watch television, that night comes back to haunt me."

2. What time of day is the most difficult for you?

_____

_____

_____

_____

_____

_____

"Going to bed," says Alice. "I will stay up as long as I can so I don't have to think about Ted not being there. A lonely bed is a terrible thing. I get up in the middle of the night and forget he's gone. Then I start crying all over again. I mean crying really hard. It's the worst."

Glenn and Cathy had prayed for a child for ten years. "At last God answered our prayers and our son was born. He was the light of our lives. He was a good kid—he did well in school, played sports, and enjoyed being with his friends. One night my wife and I had just gotten into bed. The house was quiet. Suddenly we heard an explosion that sounded like a gun shot. We ran to our son's room and the horror of what we saw could not be real. Our beloved son was slumped over his desk, blood everywhere, dead. The gun had fallen out of his hand to the floor. I remember my wife starting to scream. I think about that moment every time I crawl into bed."

3. What do you do to battle the despair? Is there a favorite place you go? Or a place you avoid? A friend you can talk with? How do you handle your darkest moments?

_____

_____

_____

_____

_____

_____

_____

"I still can't go out to the barn." Sarah's husband was in the barn fixing the wheel of a tractor when the tractor fell on him and crushed him. "If it was up to me, I'd burn that dang thing down. But we have cows and they need the barn. Our son has to go out to milk them. I just can't go in there. But I can go out to the garden. Jake made it for me for my birthday. He made a bench from a tree that had been my favorite but had gotten hit by lightning. Sitting on that bench gives me comfort. I can feel his presence there. And I can yell at him for dying," Sarah laughs.

 Healing prayer for today: Bring me out of my distress, Lord. Help me find a new purpose for my life. Come to me quickly.

DAY 6

I Am So Afraid

The Lord is my light and my salvation; whom shall I fear? The Lord is the stronghold of my life; of whom shall I be afraid?

—PSALM 27:1

The death of a loved one brings many changes, and those changes often feel terrifying. Fear can paralyze us if we let it. Yet fear is not from God. "For God did not give us a spirit of cowardice, but rather a spirit of power and of love and of self-discipline" (2 Timothy 1:7).

Over and over Jesus says, "Fear not." You hear the words but the fear still lingers, catching your very breath in its grasp. What can you do?

The disciples who knew Jesus better than any mortals were petrified at learning of his arrest. Fear drove them to run away, and even Peter denied he knew Jesus. Fear has power to lure us into doing things we might normally not do. But hear what Jesus told his beloved apostles when he saw them again: "And remember, I am with you always, to the end of the age" (Matthew 28:20).

Jesus lives. Because he is indeed your savior, you can choose to come into his presence, receive his comfort, and be released from fear. Fear will have no power over you in the presence of Christ. Does calling upon your Lord to heal you seem too easy? It is. That's his plan.

1. Describe a time when you felt very afraid.

_____

_____

_____

_____

_____

_____

_____

"I am afraid of everything," Jenny said. "Ever since my husband's death—all I see is death. I am afraid to go out because I might have a car wreck and die. I am afraid to go to sleep because I might never wake up. I am afraid to change the lightbulb because I might electrocute myself. What I am most afraid of is living any longer. I am scared because sometimes I think dying would be easier."

2. Sometimes in grief our fears don't seem logical, but that doesn't matter. Fear is fear and it can be a real emotion. List some of the fears you might be facing.

_____

_____

_____

_____

_____

_____

_____

Stacy is twenty-seven. Two years ago her husband, who was barely twenty-seven when he died, had a heart attack while jogging. "I'm the same age as Jack. All I can think about is: Am I going to die, too? It scares me to death. I think about dying all the time. I'm even afraid to go out of the house because I might get hit by a car or something, but then I'm afraid that if I don't go out, I'll die and no one will find my body. I know it's irrational, but there it is."

"You're afraid to go out, I'm afraid to go home," says Clay. "I get home and feel so depressed because Kathy is not there that I start to drink. I mean, really drink. So I work crazy long hours, just to avoid going home and possibly becoming an alcoholic."

3. While fear is often a "normal" reaction to grief, "paralyzing fear" is not healthy. If you are feeling paralyzed by your fears, what or who could help you break out of the trap?

_____

_____

_____

_____

_____

_____

"I've always been terrified of elevators," says Connie. "My husband Fred had been rushed to the hospital and was dying. He was on the fourteenth floor. I had to get on the elevator or I'd never be able to say good-bye. So I closed my eyes, held on to my son's hand, shook all the way, and did it. I won't say I got over my fear of elevators, but I did that day. I guess love conjures fear."

4. What are some healthy things you might consider doing to deal with fear?

_____

_____

_____

_____

_____

_____

"Well, I changed the damn lightbulb," laughs Jenny. "Always hated going into our dark basement and I was scared to death of getting up on a ladder. My husband always did that for me. But I had to get a suitcase from the basement. I called my niece and she went down to the basement with me and held the ladder. I feel like I climbed up a mountain and down again, but I did it. Lightbulbs no longer scare me. Basements no longer scare me. Even ladders no longer scare me. I am invincible!"

5. Fear can sometimes be triggered by situations and sometimes by environment. What time of day is it when you feel most fearful? Where were you? Were you alone or with other people? What do you think might have caused such a fear?

_____

_____

_____

_____

_____

_____

"Nighttime is the worst for me," says Sophie, whose husband of over fifty years died in his sleep. "I hear noises in the house I never noticed before. I sit in bed wondering if someone's going to break in and try to kill me. I'm an old lady, what can I do? Who's going to protect me? I am terrified most nights."

"Get a big dog!" laughs Charlie. "That's what I did. My partner, Bob, was the brave one. We'd hear a noise and off he'd go before I could even think of what to do. After he died of AIDS, I was scared to go to the door even in the daytime. A friend brought over a puppy. I named him Bob. No one ever told me the little puppy would grow up to be so big . . . or that he would eat so much," Charlie laughs. "But if Bob hears a sound in the night he barks ferociously. He'd scare any burglar away. I now sleep soundly at night with Bob at the foot of my bed."

6. Now that you have thought about it, think of some ways in which you might change your routine to lessen the chance of feeling fearful.

_____

_____

_____

_____

_____

"I hate spiders! They scare me to death. My husband always killed them for me. Well, we have these ole banana spiders where we live. About as big as a Volkswagen. Okay, maybe not that big, but close. I came home from the funeral reception and there was this big ole spider lurking on the wall. Just staring at me with little beady eyes. I ran out of the house and sat on the front porch. Then I got mad at my husband for dying. I mean really mad. I rolled up a newspaper, walked into the house, and smashed that spider to bits. I have no idea how to get the stain off the wall, but that sucker is dead!"

 Healing prayer for today: Come, Lord Jesus, let your steadfast love fill my heart and cast out my fear that I may be set free to work with you.

DAY 7

I Feel So Alone in My Grief

At three o'clock Jesus cried out with a loud voice,
"Eloi, Eloi, lema sabachthani?" which means,
"My God, my God, why have you forsaken me?"
—MARK 15:34

In the first weeks after a funeral, friends are more than willing to listen as you express your sorrow. "But where do you go when your friends are tired of hearing you cry?" asked Margaret. "It's been a year since my mother died. They tell me it's time to go on with my life. How? My friends don't understand; in fact, they seem to be avoiding me. Never in my life have I felt so totally alone."

Sadly, those who have not faced the death of a loved one can never fully understand your sense of loneliness. Grief is like a private club. You have to pay the price of membership.

Jesus paid that price. He not only felt the isolation of being rejected by the very people he came to save, but by taking on the sins of the world he became temporarily separated from God. Yet out of his great love for you and in the remembrance of his utter loneliness, he will send you others to comfort you in his name. Pray for them to arrive. Expect them and thank God when they come.

1. Has there been a time when you have felt abandoned by friends or family or even your church? Describe what happened.

_____

_____

_____

_____

_____

"I think it's because they don't know what to say." Elementary school teacher Jane's little girl was only seven when she died from leukemia. "I see the other mothers with their children at a lot of school events. I thought they were my friends since we live in the same neighborhood. I even taught some of their kids. But they never come over to talk to me, or even make the effort for eye contact. Either they don't know what to say, or they think leukemia is contagious."

2. What time of day do you feel the loneliest? What places or events make you feel all alone?

_____

_____

_____

_____

_____

_____

_____

Barry got up from the group and paced around the room. He stopped pacing and said, "I feel so isolated. I totally get the alone-on-a-deserted-island story. I am there."

"Oh, I get that!" says Katie. "I don't fit in anymore. Our friends who are couples have stopped inviting me to their parties because I am no longer a couple. People at work don't talk to me because they don't know what to say. My girlfriends were great at first but now they have their own lives to live. I know they are busy, but I am totally alone. I'm the only one on my desert."

Barry smiled and said, "It's horrible to be so alone." He began to unfold his story. He and Sonya had been together for almost ten months. They each kept their own apartments, but they had agreed they were exclusive. Sonya's family was not a happy one and after living through her parents' bitter divorce she was very leery about a relationship, not to mention marriage. "I tried so hard to love her but not smother or push her too hard" he cried out, pacing again. Then he collapsed onto a chair. "It was one night after dinner. We were settled in to watch a movie and as the opening scenes rolled by, she turned to me and said she needed to tell me something. I can still see myself hitting the pause button on the remote," he said.

"Then Sonya dropped the bomb. The past weekend she had gone on a girls-only overnight with some friends—or so I had thought. She had actually gone by herself to an abortion clinic. I still feel like I have this knot in my stomach. I feel like I can't breathe and the room starts to spin every time I talk about it."

When he found his voice, he said that all he could think to say was, "What?! Sonya sat there calmly and told me she loved me, but she certainly never intended to have children. Shouldn't we have talked about it?"

"I spiraled into a kaleidoscope of jagged edges and confusion," said Barry. "All I had were questions. Why did she lie? Why didn't she tell me? Why didn't I know? Would it have been a boy or girl? Why couldn't we have been a family? I'm forty years old. I had always wanted children. I thought we were going to get married and have a family. This might have been my last chance. This was my child, too, and she never let me decide if I wanted that child or not. She had no consideration of my feelings at all."

Barry spoke with a voice fraught with emotion. "The worst part is, I am alone in the pain of what if." Barry and Sonya broke off their relationship. His parents, whom he was not especially close to, never liked Sonya and were thrilled she was gone. His friends had no idea what had really happened so their advice was, "Hey man, lots of fish in the sea. Go snag a new one."

"The problem is," Barry continued, "I wanted a child. Not only am I mourning the betrayal, but mostly the baby I could have had. I wanted that baby. And I have no one to talk to who will understand. My parents are Catholic; they are against abortion and it would have freaked them out. My friends? To them the baby never existed. The problem," he continued, "is that I feel like a lone goldfish swimming around in a bowl. I can see out into the world but I am alone in my watery prison of pain."

 Healing prayer for today: Please, Jesus, send me other Christians who will understand the loneliness of my grief and my need to talk about my loved one. Fill my emptiness with your love. Be with me Lord, for I feel so alone.

When Grief Catches Me Off Guard

Be still, and know that I am God!
　—PSALM 46:10

Lynn decided that she no longer needed a grief support group. A year had passed since her husband had died from AIDS. She believed she was over her grief. The next week she was back, feeling rather defeated.

"I went to the grocery store," Lynn said. "My husband, Paul, used to love those little yellow marshmallow peep chicks you find at Easter. I went to the candy aisle, and there they were. Peep chicks in every color. I totally lost it! Paul will never see blue and purple peep chicks and it just broke my heart. I got caught off guard. It's like grief is this dark shadow, lurking in the background, and it popped out and slapped me right in the candy aisle!"

Just as you think you're getting better, grief can strike you all over again, making you feel as if you are making no progress. Lynn refers to the grief that catches her off guard as "Peep-Chick Moments." We all have them. They're normal. You're normal.

Yes, there will be times when grief will catch you off guard. Peep-Chick Moments happen because grief never fully goes away. Yet as Jim, an engineer grieving the death of his infant son, puts it, "The frequency, intensity, and duration become less."

Meanwhile, it might help to stay away from the candy aisle.

Linda laughs, "And the frozen food section. When my mother was on chemo, all she wanted was raspberries. I got her frozen raspberries, raspberry jam, and raspberry sherbet, anything with raspberries in it. About a week after she died, I was walking down the aisle of the grocery store with my sister and we were talking while putting things in the cart.

We were in the frozen food section and all of the sudden she looked down at the stuff I had nonchalantly put in. It was raspberries. We both just lost it. We hugged each other and just cried. We couldn't stop for a long time. The manager even came over to us to see if we were okay. So embarrassing! I didn't go back to that store for several weeks!"

1. When was a time grief caught you off guard? A time when you thought you were "over it" but discovered you weren't?

_____

_____

_____

_____

_____

Recently, Samantha returned to her hometown for the funeral of a family friend. At the graveside she turned around and there was Uncle Bubba. Uncle Bubba had the exact eyes of her beloved late mother-in-law. Jane, someone who admits she is rarely speechless, stood there with her mouth hanging open and she burst into tears. "I just stood there with tears streaming down my face. I wished the earth would open up and swallow me whole! I felt like there was a neon sign blinking over my head that read, 'Crazy Person.'"

2. Grief can sometimes make you feel as if you are losing your mind. Has this ever happen to you? How did the people around you react?

_____

_____

_____

_____

_____

"I was in a bar with my girlfriends when this really handsome man approached me. He was gorgeous. When we started to talk, I started to cry. His voice sounded the same as my late husband's. He asked me if I was okay and I said, 'No. I'm a widow.' He quickly walked away. Heck, I didn't say black widow, just widow."

3. You never really get over your grief, but it does become easier. When was a time that you felt you were really "over it" and then discovered you were still grieving?

_____

_____

_____

_____

_____

_____

"I think it was when someone sent me a photo of my son," says Mark. "Sam died in Desert Storm some years ago. Being a guy, I felt I had to be strong for my wife, all macho and stuff. So I just stuffed it in. I hadn't even cried, but I was crying on the inside. It was sort of hard on my wife because she wanted to talk about Sam. I didn't. It was too painful. Then a buddy of his sent us a photo. Sam was all decked out in Army gear, leaning against a tank and smiling that crooked smile he always had. There was a date on the back of the photo. It was the day he died. I completely lost it. It was the last picture ever taken of my son. I didn't know I could sob so hard or so loud! I guess you cry now or you cry later. But someday it catches up with you."

4. Sometimes grief catches up with you when you least expect it. What do you do when it does?

_____

_____

_____

"I don't know why people get so wigged out because someone is grieving. It's not contagious, you know," says Dennis. "Sometimes I cry, especially in church. Sometimes it just gets to me and I cry. I have made a decision about that. I'm going to stop apologizing. Why should I? My wife and son are dead. I'm sad. I'm going to be sad for a very long time. And if I cry and someone gets upset about it, well then, I guess it's their problem."

 Healing prayer for today: Help me to know, Lord that you are God and that I can rely on your strength. Grant me the grace to persevere.

DAY 9

I Wish I Had Done Things Differently

"Come to me, all you that are weary and are carrying heavy burdens, and I will give you rest. Take my yoke upon you, and learn from me; for I am gentle and humble in heart, and you will find rest for your souls. For my yoke is easy, and my burden is light."
—MATTHEW 11:28–30

Most of us who face the death of a loved one have a few regrets. We wish we had done some things better; we wish we had not done some things at all. We often assume that had we done things differently, the outcome might have changed.

The reality is we cannot relive the event, but we do have the power to change how we perceive it. We can acknowledge that we are not perfect. We did the best we could and, if given a second chance, we would have gladly done it better.

Chances are the disciples wished they had done things differently and had not betrayed Jesus. Yet when they met the risen Christ again, what did he say to them? "Peace be with you."

If there is a regret that is holding you prisoner in your grief, give it to God. Tell him what you wished you had said or done differently. And know that he will give you rest. Peace be with you, as well.

1. If you had it to do over again, how might you do things differently?

_____

_____

_____

_____

_____

_____

_____

"I wish I had learned more about our complicated finances," adds Kim. "My husband kept trying to explain everything to me, but I didn't want to think about him dying and so I kept telling him that we'd talk about it when he got better. Then he died. I knew nothing about our business, taxes, or investments or even how to pay the bills. Frank did all that. His brother helped me at the beginning, but I'm still not understanding a lot. My husband wanted to take care of me, help me to take over the business, but I missed that opportunity. I really wish I had listened to him."

"I would have told my husband I loved him," says Sandy. "We were going to the beach for the day to go diving. I had packed a lunch and remembered I forgot the mayonnaise. We were on a mountain road in South America that leads to the beach when a boulder came down from the mountain and crushed our car. My husband died instantly but I came out with only a few scratches. My last words to him were, 'I forgot the damn mayonnaise!' That's not what I would have said if I had known those were our last moments together. I would have told him I loved him"

2. Is there anything you wish you had said to your loved one before he or she died?

_____

_____

_____

_____

_____

_____

"I know this is silly but I wish I had told my grandmother how much money I make," says Abigail. "She asked me. And I didn't tell her. It mattered to her. All her life she scrimped and saved for her family. I guess she wanted to make sure I was going to be okay. I didn't tell her. I make a really good salary. I wish I had told her that."

3. Sometimes we carry around guilt for things said and not said, done and not done. Is guilt one of those things that haunt you? If so, confess it now and God, being so loving, will forgive you and release you.

_____

_____

_____

_____

_____

_____

Diane worked as a counselor in a veterans' hospital. PTSD was a common problem that plagued many of her patients. Diane often prayed silently for the people with whom she worked, but because it was a state-funded institution she was not allowed to talk about her faith for any reason whatsoever.

One afternoon she was working with Chuck, an older man who had been stationed in Vietnam in the sixties. He had lived through the Tet Offensive of 1968 that killed many of his friends. A mass grave had been found in the city of Hue. His unit had been assigned to help recover the bodies of the dead and transport them to the set-up morgue.

Diane says, "As always, on that afternoon Chuck's eyes were dull and he exuded complete despair. Some days he would not speak at all during the sessions, responding only with a shrug or a nod of his head. That afternoon the inspectors for the yearly review of the facility were also on campus. The comprehensive review included time spent evaluating each employee as well as the client logs and progress reports. They were watching to see how we dealt with clients."

"Chuck and I were sitting in the rec room," Diane stated. "I was nervous because I was aware the inspectors were in the room observing myself and two other coworkers. Chuck seemed even more withdrawn than usual," Diane mused. "I was working through the treatment plan when suddenly Chuck leaned toward me and said, 'pray for me.'" Diane flinched as she continued, "I looked around to see where the inspectors were and then I leaned into Chuck and reminded him that I could not do that. I was so afraid," she added, "that the inspectors would hear."

That night Diane replayed the episode in her mind and again as she dressed for work the next morning. She resolved she would find some way to pray with Chuck. When she arrived at work and put her things away, she checked in with the front desk for her schedule. She glanced down and did not see Chuck's name. She went to find her supervisor to ask about him. Her supervisor responded that Chuck had killed himself last night. Diane reeled with shock. Then she said she heard her supervisor's voice as though it was coming from far away. "I could not understand what she was saying," Diane could scarcely get out. And then she said, "I heard my supervisor saying, 'And so you have nothing to worry about. The inspectors gave you a superior rating.'"

"A superior rating, when I am responsible for that dear man's death. I will never forgive myself for not praying for him when he asked me to."

 Healing prayer for today: Lord I am not perfect, but you are. Please forgive me for anything I may have done or said that I now regret. Release me from my guilt as only you can.

I Can't Forgive Myself

All the prophets testify about him that everyone
who believes in him receives forgiveness of sins
through his name.
    —Acts 10:43

"I keep going through the whole thing in my mind," said Don. "What if
I had said 'no' when the doctor asked to remove my wife from the ventilator? I wish I had said 'no.' I know what the doctors told me, that she
was brain dead and there was no sense in keeping her on a machine. But
I feel responsible for her death by giving permission to turn it off, and I
can't forgive myself for that."

What a difficult decision Don had to make. Yes, perhaps if he had not
given permission, his wife's body would still be here. But her soul was
trapped in that shell that was once his dear Barbara. Out of compassion
and faith and with great selfless courage, Don released her to her Lord.
Still, he can't help but wonder if he did the right thing, and the memory
of that decision haunts him.

Is there anything you regret doing or saying before your loved one
died? Most people have some regrets. Now that your loved one is gone,
it's too late to ask for forgiveness. Or is it? At the death of Jesus, surely
the disciples anguished in their guilt brought on by denying him. If only
they had not been weak. If only they had shown their love for him and
stood by him. If only they had . . . the list goes on, as it might for you.

The disciples not only were able to be forgiven by the physical presence of Christ himself, but they were able to forgive themselves through
the abundant love of his mercy. That same gentle power of forgiveness
is but a breath away for you as well. Through the presence of the Holy
Spirit Jesus left behind, you can be forgiven. Just ask.

There is nothing that is unforgivable. The burden you carry is not too heavy for your Lord to bear. Leave your regrets at the foot of his cross.

1. When it comes to forgiveness, what things do you wish to have forgiven?

_____

_____

_____

_____

_____

_____

_____

"My wife had her first heart attack, a relatively mild one, five years before her death. Our lives changed dramatically. Our diet and exercise plan took on a new dimension. We went to the YMCA and took a CPR class. We studied relaxation techniques and took any step we could think of to 'de-stress' our lives. I loved her dearly, but I tell you—I killed my wife."

George is haunted by the memory of his wife's death and he cannot forgive himself. "On the night she died, I woke up to go the bathroom. As I came back to bed I glanced over at her and something did not seem right. I shook her gently with fear rising in my throat. Shaking so hard I could barely get the light on as I realized I was screaming at her. I somehow managed to call 911 and remembered my CPR training."

"Through a cloudy lens I remember seeing my wife on the gurney, bright red ambulance lights and sounds I could not recognize. I have no idea how I got to the hospital. It seemed I had just set foot in the emergency room door and I realized a white-coated person was looking for me. My heart raced. I remember thinking I should have brought her meds with me."

"What was he saying to me? Karen. Dead. It can't be possible. I did CPR. Then the awful reality set in. I killed Karen because I did not do the CPR right."

2. Guilt, by definition, is the concept that we did something wrong, our actions were wrong. Some refer to guilt as anger turned inward. Is there something surrounding the death of your loved one for which you need to forgive yourself? How might you ask God to help you?

_____

_____

_____

_____

_____

_____

Allen wanted to share first that evening. "Man, this is what I can't get past. Our three amigos group had gone on our annual fishing trip. We had gone to Alaska for the salmon season. Whew. We were slaying them. It had been the best trip ever." Allen stopped and fiddled with the pencil in his hand. "At dinner that night," he began, "Derik announced he was dying and this would be his last fishing trip." With tears in his eyes, Allen looked up and said, "I laughed. I told him no way, give it up." He looked at the pencil and snapped it. "Derik was dead two months later. Why did I laugh?"

3. Forgiving doesn't always mean forgetting. How might you forgive yourself, and not let the memory haunt you?

_____

_____

_____

_____

_____

_____

"I beat myself up pretty bad after my stepfather died," says Marci. "We were in the car crash together. He was flung from the car because he wasn't using a seat belt. For months I felt it was my fault. He had taken his seatbelt off at the stoplight to reach in the back to get me a bottle of water. He forgot to put it back on. I blamed myself for months. If only I hadn't asked him for that bottle of water! My mother helped me to realize that it was the guy who ran the stoplight who was at fault, and that my stepfather would have died anyway because of the way the car hit us. But I carried around that guilt for a long time."

4. If you haven't as yet, could you ask God to forgive you now? What would you like to say to him?

_____

_____

_____

_____

_____

_____

Marjorie sighs. "After my husband died I had such guilt. Tremendous guilt. I had been unfaithful to George about ten years ago. It wasn't a long affair, but I betrayed him. I finally went to see my priest. She told me to give my guilt to God and had me write out my confession before we went into the church. Then we prayed and I put the confession on the altar. After she gave me absolution, she took my hand and said, 'Now go and sin no more'. I felt as if Jesus himself was giving me forgiveness. That confession totally released me."

5. If you have already asked God for help, have you seen evidence of his forgiveness?

_____

_____

_____

_____

_____

_____

Joyce and her brother had had a big fight just before Jim was killed in a freak football accident. "We were always fighting. I loved my brother but felt awful that I never told him. I prayed to God that he would tell Jim I loved him. A few months later, when we cleaned out his room, we found a box of photos he had taken. There was one of me. On the back Jim had written, 'Love this kid. She'll tear you apart if you cross her. But I'm safe 'cuz she loves me.'"

 Healing prayer for today: Forgive me, Lord. Forgive me for things said or unsaid; things done or left undone. I leave my remorse at the foot of your cross and thank you that you are the Lord of mercy, forgiveness, and abundant love.

DAY 11

I'm So Mad!

Be angry but do not sin; do not let the sun go down
on your anger, and do not make room for the devil.
—Ephesians 4:26–27

As Christians, if we truly love the Lord, we should never become angry, right? Nonsense! Even Jesus got angry.

"I'm not the type who gets angry," says Erica, who is mourning the death of her brother. "But I am so angry! I have this rage inside of me and I don't know what to do with it."

To be angry that her cherished brother Mark was murdered during a robbery is not only a valid emotion but also a natural reaction. Anger during grief is common and to be expected. It is often enhanced if the death is caused by a violent crime, suicide, or medical malpractice. Sometimes we aren't sure with whom we're angry. We might be furious at the doctors who couldn't save our loved one or the nurse who didn't give a loved one tender loving care. We can be angry with ourselves for not doing more and even feel anger at the one who died. How *dare* the person leave us! And sometimes we become angry with God. Why didn't he intervene?

You are not a bad Christian for feeling angry. Anger in itself is not a sin. In fact, Paul says in Ephesians, "Be angry." The first step in not letting "the sun go down on your anger" is to admit that you are enraged. Anger denied does not go away. It wells up in us, festers and comes out in bitterness or even vengeance. That anger can even cause us to harm ourselves or others. Where the sin lies is in what we do about the rage inside us. Erica and her family used the energy from their anger to develop a foundation in her brother's name that gives scholarships to less fortunate students. Their actions defeated anger, defeated the evil that caused her brother's death, honored Mark, and gave glory to God in the process.

1. What is something that makes you angry?

_____

_____

_____

_____

_____

_____

"I am not mad," Brad said. As he said it, his voice started to rise and his hands curled into fists. His visible agitation rose as he repeated, "I am not mad. I AM NOT ANGRY. I loved my wife." Finally screaming he said, "AND I AM NOT ANGRY I FOUND HER STASH OF CIGARETTES EVEN THOUGH SHE SWORE TO ME SHE HAD QUIT SMOKING!"

Brad later admitted that he felt betrayed by his wife, who died from lung cancer, smoking until the bitter end. Brad did not believe he could be angry without dishonoring his wife's memory. But until he could admit his frustration and resentment, he was stuck in that angry place.

2. It's okay to feel anger with a loved one who has died. Is there something or someone with whom you are angry?

_____

_____

_____

_____

_____

_____

"A heart attack at thirty-six? Who has a heart attack at thirty-six?" asks Beth. "We have five kids and now I have to raise them alone. Why would God do this? I'm so damn mad at him! In fact, I thought my hate was going to eat me up. My minister came to my house and asked why I hadn't been to church. I told him I was mad as hell at God. When he told me it was okay, that God had big shoulders, and that put me at ease.

When I told him why, he understood and told me that being mad at God was an act of faith; that God was real and it was okay to be mad at him. That really helped. I'm still angry at him, but not as much. At least I know that it's okay to tell him when I'm mad at him."

3. Are you angry with God? It's okay if you are. If so, tell him about it.

_____

_____

_____

_____

_____

_____

"Well, I'm not angry at God, I'm just angry at his behavior," said Georgia. After a long pause she screamed, "Okay fine, I'm really ticked off with God! Boy that felt better."

In the days after September 11, 2001, many people were angry with God. "Why didn't he stop it? Does God hate us? How come some people lived and others didn't? I'm so angry with God that I've lost my faith."

While God is not responsible for such evil, Jesus weeps with us when such horrific things occur. And it's okay to be mad at him. It isn't a lack of faith, it's a proof of faith that God exists. Besides, he has big shoulders. He can take it.

"I felt bad talking to God the way I did. I told him I hated him for taking my little boy. For making him suffer for so long. I shouted how much I hated him for days. After the things I said to him, I figured he must hate me, too."

God understands your anger. Remember, Jesus got angry, too . . . flipping tables in the temple like a New Jersey Housewife. He loves your loved one as much as you do and even more, if you can imagine that. It was never his plan that anyone would die. Even in death, Jesus is there to receive those we cherish into the kingdom of heaven and to keep them safe until we meet again.

 Healing prayer for today: Lord God, help me to face and confess my anger and then take it from me. Help me to find something constructive I may do with this hurtful energy. Use my anger for your glory.

Feeling Bad for Feeling Good

> For everything there is a season, and a time for
> every matter under heaven: a time to be born, and
> a time to die; a time to plant, and a time to pluck
> up what is planted; a time to kill, and a time to
> heal; a time to break down, and a time to build
> up; a time to weep, and a time to laugh; a time
> to mourn, and a time to dance.
> —ECCLESIASTES 3:1–4

"For months after the death of my mother, I cried every day," says Janice. "Then one day I didn't. I went a whole day without crying. You'd think I'd be happy about that, but I wasn't. I felt guilty. How could I not be sad that my mother is dead? I felt like such a rotten daughter."

If we truly believe, and we do, that our resurrected life with our Lord will be filled with unbelievable happiness; and if we believe, and we do, that love gives our mortal lives happiness, then we must come to the conclusion that happiness is the will of God. While it may not seem like it now, there will come a time when you will laugh again. You may even go through a day when you don't even think about your loved one. Does that mean you didn't love enough? No, it simply means your Lord loves you more.

Soaking in grief will not bring your loved one back. Remembering the joy you once shared, and then carrying on the legacy to share that remembered happiness with others, pays tribute to a Lord of love and to the memory of your loved one. There is a time to laugh and a time to dance. Rejoice in knowing that our God is an awesome God. Jesus has the supernatural power to save us from the depths of despair and the power to bring us to joy once more. *That* is a healing miracle!

1. Describe a day, when your loved one was alive, that was one of the best days the two of you shared. What made it so special? When you think of that day, does the remembrance make you smile?

_____

_____

_____

_____

_____

_____

"We had gone hiking in the Blue Ridge Parkway. Everything was perfect. The weather was cool. The trails were empty except for us. We sat down for lunch when this deer came to get a drink from the creek. Then came her two babies. We were very quiet and watched them a long time. It was sweet and such a precious moment for us until my husband whispered, 'Do you like venison? I think I can get her with one shot.' That ruined the whole moment. But I think about that day every time I see a deer, and yes, it does make me smile."

2. Everyone has foibles or little idiosyncrasies that are unique to them. Describe one your loved one had. While it might have driven you crazy at the time, remembering them now, do they make you smile?

_____

_____

_____

_____

_____

_____

"My wife used to snap her gum," says Rob. "Drove me insane. Snap, snap, snap. The other day I was standing in line at Walmart and there was a woman behind me snapping her gum for all it's worth. Her husband asked her to stop, just I like used to do. Then she whips her head toward him and says, 'I'm not snapping! Geez. Can't a girl just enjoy her gum?' That's exactly what my wife used to say. I laughed, I mean really laughed. And then got a dirty look from the girl."

3. It is God's plan for you to be happy again, so why might you suddenly feel guilty or sad when you start feeling happy again?

_____

_____

_____

_____

_____

_____

_____

Kathy's child died at the age of two from leukemia. "Maybe it's because when I feel happy about something, I remember that my daughter will never get to experience the things that make kids happy. She never got to have Christmas at home, or go to an attraction. We had planned to go to Disney World, but she was too sick. I don't ever want to forget my daughter. If I start feeling happy, it scares me into thinking that I will forget her."

4. Could it be possible that God brings you happy moments in your grief because of his love for you? Can grief be so painful that he sends you a respite?

_____

_____

_____

_____

_____

_____

_____

"My friend shared with me over a cup of coffee that she made sure she cried at least once a day since her mother died eighteen months ago. There was a reason why, she explained. A few weeks earlier, without realizing it, she had gone an entire day without crying. Her husband noticed and made the remark, 'Hey, you must be getting better, you didn't cry today.' She looked at me and said, 'I am afraid I won't always feel good, so I make sure that I cry at least once a day . . . in front of my husband.'"

5. Describe a time when the day ended and you realized you felt good.

_____

_____

_____

_____

_____

_____

"It was bath time," Ruby said. "I realized I had played with the kids, made bubbles, scrubbed them with their favorite green dinosaur bath mitt and sung the pirate on the ocean song, and I had not once felt pain. My husband, Roger, had first instituted the pirate song." Ruby lingered in a past memory. She began again, "I did not ever think I could hear, much less sing the pirate song after he died. When I first realized what I had done, I couldn't believe I had sung it. But now, I feel such a peace. Gee," she added, "I would never have thought that could happen."

 Healing prayer for today: Almighty God and Father, thank you for returning me to joy once more, as my loved one is blissfully in the presence of your Son and the whole company of heaven. Thank you that I can become joyful again through the power of your mercy.

DAY 13

Is It Okay to Feel Relieved that My Loved One Is Gone?

When they call to me, I will answer them;
I will be with them in trouble, I will rescue
them and honor them.
    —Psalms 91:15

"Why won't God let me die? I can't stand this pain anymore. Please tell him to let me die!"

Tom was in excruciating pain from cancer and near death. Yet death was elusive. His family was frantic to give him release and even considered giving him an overdose to put an end to his suffering. But Jesus had a better plan. Tom needed to let go of unfinished business in this life before he could enter the next. God in his mercy allowed the man time to heal some brokenness. Tom left this life, not in physical or spiritual torment, but in peace. Surrounded by those who loved him, Tom was joyfully released to God, who loves him most.

Letting go of your loved ones is not easy, it takes selfless courage. Yearning for a release from this life for those who suffer does not mean you are lax in your love for them. In fact, it shows great compassion and faith. God does not "take" our loved ones from this life, but rescues and lovingly receives them once they have died. You may go forth in peace, rejoicing that it was your faith that set them free and trusting that it was your Lord who gave them eternal refuge. Free from pain. Free from sorrow.

1. It's okay to feel some relief when a loved one dies. You're exhausted from watching them in pain, or you're just plain exhausted. Wanting release does not mean you didn't love. Was there a moment when you just wished that they would go?

_____

_____

_____

_____

_____

_____

"You're going to think I'm horrible, but I couldn't wait for my husband to die, not because I hated seeing him suffer. He had always been abusive. Beat me constantly. Never gave me any money. Never helped with the kids. He'd just get drunk and take it out of me and the boys. When we found out he had liver failure I counted the days until he'd die. I loved him, but frankly, I'm glad the old goat is gone."

"I took a plane to see my grandmother. My cousins called me to say she was dying. She had congestive heart failure and would gag constantly. I hated seeing her that way. When I got there, all of a sudden she began to rally and seemed better. But that didn't last long. The next day she began to suffer all over again. Medicine didn't help. She was a very gentle woman and was always helping others. Why couldn't God help her now? Why couldn't she go off in peace without suffering? I noticed her blood pressure was dropping and I just wished and prayed that she'd just go. I felt so guilty about feeling like that, but I couldn't stand that she was suffering."

2. Sometimes the prolonged death process can really unravel a family. Family dynamics come to the forefront and can get ugly. How did your family handle the moments leading up to the death of your loved one?

_____

_____

_____

_____

_____

_____

"There is no 'fun' in my dysfunctional family. I still cringe when I remember my dad's death. I was trying to hold everything together. Dad had been sick with cancer for so long. An entire end of our home was turned into a hospital ward. Hospice brought a bed that was in the middle of the living room. Other hospital equipment was scattered all around. Medical charts, extra diapers, blood pressure cuff, etc., were all stacked on an end table. The lingering smell of sickness never faded. Hospice came twice a day, but for some reason Dad never was out of pain. He moaned and cried out constantly."

"Two days before he died we realized my younger sister had figured out a way to steal the pain drugs and was selling them. I went crazy. I called the police and had her arrested. The circus got even crazier, but at least Dad got some pain relief. The moment of dad's last breath, I closed my eyes as relief flooded through me. Relief, not only for me, but also for him. All I could think is that, 'At last it is over. Thank you, God that it is over.' That was three years ago and I still feel relieved, although I miss my Dad still."

3. Family members, in frustration or good intentions, can say or do something that makes things worse. Did that happen in your case?

_____

_____

_____

_____

_____

_____

"My brother's an idiot, and I mean that in the nicest way, but he's a real moron! When dad was dying and in a lot of pain, my brother brought marijuana to the hospital room. He starts rolling one in front of the family. Everybody went nuts and started screaming at him. But I get it. Mitchell is a very frail person and couldn't stand watching our dad in pain. He was just trying to help the best he knew how. But what an idiot."

 Healing prayer for today: Look mercifully on me, Lord, for I am in great distress. Help me to let go and to be free from any remorse. Receive my loved one into your presence and fill my emptiness with your love.

DAY 14

Grief Makes Me Sick

Great crowds came to him, bringing with them the
lame, the maimed, the blind, the mute, and many
others. They put them at his feet, and he cured them.
—MATTHEW 15:30

Just getting out of bed in the morning can be a great victory while in the midst of grief. "Good Morning" can seem like a trick question. "Grief feels more like the flu than anything else," says Robert. "I was in pretty good physical shape before my wife died. I ran every day, worked out, and was a high-energy kind of guy. Now I feel like a truck has run over me. I can't seem to get any energy at all. Am I always going to feel like this?"

While grief can cause complete exhaustion, you are not doomed to be lethargic for the rest of your life. Eventually you will begin to feel better physically, just not right away. Symptoms of grief often feel like you're coming down with something. Your blood pressure may rise. You may feel as if you are having heart flutters. You may develop a cold that won't go away, a thirst that can't be quenched, indigestion, a rash, muscle tightness, or shaking. There are many other physical ailments that can be caused or heightened by grief.

Contacting your physician is a good idea. Contacting your Great Physician is also wise. Perhaps the listlessness you are feeling is your Lord's way of telling you to slow down for a while and to be kind to yourself. Give yourself time to heal from grief just as if you had a disease or, in this case, a dis-ease. In the meantime, take refuge in the arms of your Lord. Spend time with him through prayer and the reading of Scriptures. Surrender to God, who alone has the power to heal you and give you rest, and he will restore you.

1. In your grief, have you felt different physically? How so?

_____

_____

_____

_____

_____

_____

"Right after my mother died I developed a cough. I couldn't shake it even with antibiotics. I went back to the doctor and she took a chest X-ray. When she put it up to the light box, it hit me. It was the same light box where we looked at my mother's X-ray and found the cancer. It was weird, right then and there my cough went away. I think I was coughing because she did."

"I had the same experience!" says Joan. "I thought my doctor would think I was crazy. Shoot, I think I am crazy about half the time. I also had a cough that wouldn't go away. I called my doctor to schedule another chest X-ray. I had already had one and it was clear, but I told the doctor, 'This time it is real, I think I have a cancerous lump and it will show up. My coughing will not stop and I feel awful.' I patiently waited while the tech adjusted the X-ray machine. I had a strange sense of calm. Death won't be so bad, I thought. At least I will stop this constant coughing. The doctor flipped the light on the wall and illuminated the X-ray for me. He asked me, 'Joan, what do you see?' 'Coughing,' I said. He said, 'What we have here is a perfectly healthy set of lungs.' 'Then why am I coughing all the time?' I asked in disbelief. Time wore on and I continued to cough. Two years to the day of my sister's death I stopped coughing. I connect my cough to my sister. She died of lung cancer."

2. When we are in grief the body grieves as well, and we can exhibit physical symptoms. The symptoms may even be the same type that led to the death of our loved one. Have you felt any symptoms mimicking those of your loved one?

_____

_____

_____

_____

_____

_____

_____

"For me," says Victor, "It was a pain in my back. I had gone to many doctors to figure out what the problem was. None of them ever found anything. But I was in real pain. I mean it hurt! Finally, one doctor asked if I had had anyone in my family die recently. I thought it was a strange question. I told him my brother had been stabbed in a barroom brawl. He asked me if there had been a knife wound to his back. Yes, Hector had been stabbed in the back. That's when it came to me. I had always taken care of my little brother but not that night. After talking to a counselor, the pain eventually went away."

3. What physical symptoms have you felt or are you feeling now that may be related to grief?

_____

_____

_____

_____

_____

_____

_____

"I feel lightheaded a lot," says Liz. "And sometimes nauseated."

"I still have a headache that won't go away," says Russ.

"I thought I was having a heart attack," says Roger. "My wife made me go to the doctor, but I was just fine."

 Healing prayer for today: I submit myself to you, dear Lord. Come close to me, Jesus, and heal my physical pain and disease. Restore me to your perfect health so that I may dwell in you and you in me.

DAY 15

Am I Losing My Mind?

Your eyes will see strange things, and your mind
utter perverse things. You will be like one who lies
down in the midst of the sea, like one who lies on
the top of a mast.
—PROVERBS 23:33–34

There are moments when grief makes you feel as though you are going mad. Do you wonder if you will ever be able to think clearly again? Do you have moments when you fear you are losing your mind? Have you walked into a room and been unable to remember why and then couldn't even remember what room you were in? Do you forget people's names, how to pronounce words, or where you put things?

These symptoms are common to all who grieve. "I thought I was losing my mind," says Dorothy. "I was worried I was developing Alzheimer's until I learned that forgetfulness can be caused by grief. What a relief! I'm not crazy."

Grief can feel like insanity. One moment you're sad, the next highly agitated or euphoric. You cry at the drop of a hat, or have unexplained bouts of dread. You're moody, restless, critical, and suspicious. You have difficulty concentrating; you're forgetful, have complete memory loss, and can't get anything accomplished when once you were highly productive.

Does any of this sound familiar? While you may feel as if you have become uncharacteristically unstable, you have not. These symptoms are familiar to most people who grieve. The good news is these symptoms are temporary. And while it may seem as if you are lost in a fog with no lantern, you are progressing through the haze. Grief takes time. The light that is willing to guide you back to safety is your Lord. Trust him.

1. Have you had moments when you really thought you were losing your mind? What happened to make you feel that way?

_____

_____

_____

_____

_____

_____

A slight sheepish expression on his face, John said in a low voice, "I think I am going crazy, like I mean certifiable, white jacket kind of crazy." John began to explain about some of the things that were happening to him. "I put the coffee creamer in the microwave instead of the refrigerator. At work I could not remember a client's name and almost lost one of our biggest accounts. Friends had asked me to dinner and I showed up two nights before I was supposed to. Yesterday I spent an hour trying to find my car keys that were sitting on top of the washing machine. I have no idea about that," he said.

Desperate in tone now, he related that he had "gone off like a rocket" on a colleague who told a joke at lunch. "And this was one of my closest work friends. I must really be crazy," he said again, "because I don't even know this person I am now."

"I'm a psychiatric nurse and I thought I should just Baker Act myself onto the ward," says Angie. "There are days when I just want to go home, get my PJs, come back to the ward, and eat lime gelatin."

Angie had put her infant daughter to bed, and then went to bed herself. She heard the baby fuss a little, but then she seemed to fall asleep quickly. The next morning she went in to check on her baby. That's when she realized the child had died in the night from SIDS.

"I know it's impossible, but I hear her little voice every night. I keep hearing her cry. I wake up in the middle of the night shouting, 'Mommy is coming!' I mean, how do you get over something like that?"

Gayle says, "My husband was killed in the Gulf War. I never got to say good-bye to him. Everywhere I go I see someone who looks like him and I think it's him. Same build, same walk, even his blond curly hair. I run up to complete strangers and shout, 'Leonard?' I've really got to stop doing that or I'm going to get arrested."

2. It is not unusual to think you have seen your loved ones walking down the street, or you seem to hear their voice, or even think you feel their presence. While we know our loved one is no longer here, these occurrences can seem very real and sometimes scary. The good news is that you are truly not crazy, you are in grief and this is common and natural. Has this happened to you?

_____

_____

_____

_____

_____

_____

_____

"I could not even tell the kids," Kevin said in a near whisper. "Even Charlie, our lab who sleeps with me, looked at me like I was a candidate for the Krazy Kennel Klub." As Kevin's story unfolded, many heads around the table began to nod in agreement. Kevin had been reading before bed. "This house was quiet and suddenly I heard Lisette singing her brush your teeth song," he said. Kevin expanded the story by explaining that he had always teased Lisette for singing while she brushed her teeth. Lisette had always just laughed and said it was how she gauged if she had brushed long enough. Kevin looked up and said, "I actually got up and went into the bathroom. I knew she was there and this nightmare was over. I even looked in the closet. It was so real."

"I can smell my mother. I can walk into a room and smell her perfume. She wore Aphrodisiac," says Renee. "No one's made that perfume in over fifty years, but I can sometimes smell her."

 Healing prayer for today: Gracious Lord, I ask you to heal my body, mind, and spirit. For I am feeling lost and I need you to show me the way. Grant me a clear mind, so that I may think of you and your mercies ever more clearly.

DAY 16

Will I Ever Stop Crying?

My eyes will flow without ceasing, without respite,
until the Lord from heaven looks down and sees.
— LAMENTATIONS 3:49–50

During the first weeks of a bereavement group, Holly could not speak. All she could manage were tears. "I was afraid that I would never stop crying. However, I found a safe place where I could go to cry and that's what I did. You know what happened? Eventually the tears stopped."

When King David learned his infant son was dying, he too could not be consoled. He cried, fasted, and prayed for God to spare his child. When the baby died, David got up, stopped his crying, and began to eat. Those around the king were confused. David explained, "But now he is dead; why should I fast? Can I bring him back again? I shall go to him, but he will not return to me" (2 Samuel 12:23).

Weeping will not bring our loved ones back to us, but shedding tears can bring the memory of them closer to us. When we cry, we acknowledge the love once shared. Crying is not a lack of faith, but a release from sorrow. Tears are God's grace to us for the purpose of allowing his healing to begin. "You have kept count of my tossings; put my tears in your bottle. Are they not in your record?" (Psalm 56:8).

We know that we will see our loved ones again someday, but they are not with us now and for that we cry. Although it may seem as though you may never stop crying, no one can cry forever; it's physically impossible. During the Victorian era, small glass bottles were used to catch tears. The thought was that once the bottle was filled, the pain would be over. There is no known record of anyone filling a bottle. Let the tears flow. Think of them as Holy water, a healing balm for your soul.

1. Do you ever feel like you will never stop crying? What seems to start the tears?

_____

_____

_____

_____

_____

_____

_____

By the third week of the grief group, everyone knew to pass Ellen the box of tissues. Her beloved brother Tommy had been killed in Iraq nine months before. After the opening prayer, she took a deep breath and said, "I am an utter failure. My crying happened all week long. Last Sunday I ran out of the church crying when the organ started playing Amazing Grace."

Monday she went to her son's soccer game and sobbed through the National Anthem. Ellen said, "My son had a look on his face like he wanted to crawl into a hole. Last Tuesday I was afraid to go out of the house because I couldn't stop crying. On Wednesday I decided to push myself to go out. I was just fine but then I broke down at the nail salon because they had the TV set for the midday news and it was all about the war in the Middle East," she continued. "Will I ever stop crying? It has been nine months. What is wrong with me?"

2. Describe when crying caught you off guard.

_____

_____

_____

_____

_____

_____

"I was in my classroom," says Alice. "I teach high school literature. We were reading *Les Misérables* and one of the students was reading aloud. I don't know what happened, but all of a sudden I thought about my mother's death and lost it. I felt bad for the student because I think he thought he had caused it. Funny, but when I saw the look on his face I felt dreadful and that stopped my crying."

3. What helps comfort you when you can't stop crying?

"My dad's shirt," says Carrie. "It still smells like him. When I can't stop crying I hold onto his shirt and smell him. He would always comfort me and say, 'It's okay darling. Daddy's here.' I can almost hear him saying that and it soothes me."

"I read the psalms. I can always find comfort in them," says Randy. "Funny, I never even read them before."

"I drink wine," laughs Jean. "Not the kind you think. When I can't stop crying and feel just retched, I go to communion. When the priest says, 'with all the company of heaven,' I feel closer to my dad. He was a priest, too. I feel we are receiving communion at the same time. And that helps."

 Healing prayer for today: Please hold me close, Lord, and catch my tears. Then, in your mercy, refill my bottle with joy once more.

Why Did God Do This to Me?

And the Lord restored the fortunes of Job when
he had prayed for his friends; and the Lord gave
Job twice as much as he had before.
　　—Job 42:10

"I'm not mad at God," said Barbara. "I'm just mad at God's behavior."

One of the most thought-provoking books in the Bible is the Book of Job. Here is the story of a man, devoted servant of God, who loses everything. His wife and children die. His house is destroyed and his great wealth is dissolved. Yet throughout all his torments, Job continues to be faithful to God. That doesn't mean that Job doesn't get angry with God. He does and complains loudly that God has not been fair.

Job asks the same question we all ask in our anguish: How can God be just when we who are faithful suffer and those who are wicked are not punished? Still, the question we must ask is not why, but what? What does Job do in his suffering? He turns to God and asks God, "What happens next?" Then Job asks God to help him endure as he turns to God for comfort. What does God do for Job? He restores everything Job once had with double measure.

We may never know why our loved one died. But we can decide what to do with the pain. We can go to God for comfort. He will be there, blessing us twice fold.

Doug and Janet sat on the sofa. Janet cried softly and never looked up. Through clenched teeth Doug told the story. "Our daughter and a group of kids were on the playground at school. A drunk driver crashed through the fence killing five children, including our precious little girl. But that's not all. Three months later our son Michael was also dead.

He and three friends had found a gun that belonged to one of the boy's father. They thought it would be 'cool' to pretend to play Russian roulette like they had seen in a spy movie on TV. When it was Michael's turn, he was not 'cool,' he was stone cold dead."

"I don't understand," cries Janet. "Why would God do this to us? Why God? Why?"

1. Are you struggling with the "why"? What is the most difficult part? Do you sometimes feel like Job?

_____

_____

_____

_____

_____

"I ask why every time I try to get our twins to bed," says Davin. "I didn't even know that women died in childbirth these days. What kind of God puts a man in charge of two premature babies? I don't have a clue what I'm doing. I do thank God for sending family and friends to help. The twins are now a year old and are a great comfort to me. Kind of like in the story of Job when God restores his family. I still don't know what I'm doing, but I'm getting the hang of it. I'm a pro at diaper changing— bet Job didn't have to do that!"

2. God restored everything that Job lost. What would God have to do to restore what you have lost?

_____

_____

_____

_____

_____

_____

"We had four babies who died just after birth," says Gary. "Finally we had Victoria. We named her that because we felt that God gave us a victory. Do we still miss our other children? Absolutely. Will we ever get over the death of our other babies? No, but we can take solace that we have Victoria."

 Healing prayer for today: Almighty and merciful Father, you did not cause my suffering. Look at me with pity and heal my sorrowful heart. Restore my soul and my life, for I put my trust in you.

Can God Heal My Pain?

He himself bore our sins in his body on the cross, so
that, free from sins, we might live for righteousness;
by his wounds you have been healed.
  —1 PETER 2:24

The Gospel is filled with stories of people asking Jesus to heal them.
Out of all those who requested, guess how many he actually healed? All
of them! Not because they were deserving, not because they were righ-
teous, but simply because they asked him. Out of his love for us, and his
endless compassion, our Jesus heals the same today as he did more than
two thousand years ago.

"I know Jesus healed people when he walked the earth," says Jerry.
"But the day of miracles is over. Isn't it?"

To say that the day of miracles is over is to say that Jesus died on the
cross, which he did, but that he lost his divine power there, which he
did not. Jesus rose again, replete with supernatural power. In fact, he left
the power of his Holy Spirit with us when he breathed on his disciples
in order for them to continue the work of his ministry.

How do we know that God continues to heal some two thousand
years later? How do we know that our Lord has given us his power to
heal one another in his name? Because he said so. Jesus even left us
instructions as to how to go about asking for his healing, which can
include the healing of grief: "Are any among you sick? They should call
for the elders of the church and have them pray over them, anointing
them with oil in the name of the Lord. The prayer of faith will save the
sick, and the Lord will raise them up; and anyone who has committed
sins will be forgiven" (James 5:14–15).

Jesus does not heal with pixie dust, but by faith through prayer and
by the power of his Holy Spirit. His will for you is that you will be
restored to full health, body, mind, and spirit. How much faith does it
take? A teeny, weeny bit. Only the amount it takes to ask. Do you have a
teeny bit of faith? Then you have enough.

1. Questioning your faith is not unusual after the death of a loved one. Has the death of your loved one ever challenged your faith? How so?

_____

_____

_____

_____

_____

_____

"I guess I held God accountable for a very long time. I just couldn't accept that it was my fault that my little boy died," says Daryl. "I'm the one who left the truck running while I went inside the house to get my briefcase. Kenny got into the truck and put it into neutral. The truck slid down our hill. A car was coming around the corner, way too fast, and hit our truck with Kenny in it. He died instantly. I blamed God, I blamed the other driver, and I blamed myself. The worse thing was, I couldn't pray. We were people who went to church every Sunday and I couldn't pray."

2. God heals us even if we are undeserving. Have you ever felt you were undeserving?

_____

_____

_____

_____

_____

_____

Matt put his head in his hands and said, "I don't think God can heal my pain and I certainly don't deserve to be healed. There is no escaping the pain and I guess is it my punishment for the rest of my life."

Matt had been teaching his little sister Lisa to sail on the lake near their parents' house. Lisa had been so excited to learn. He remembers she asked him the night before the accident if she could "hold the ropes" the next day. Matt described the day as pretty at the outset, but a storm came up quickly. Matt shared that at first he was not worried; he knew they both had life vests on and they were good swimmers.

"The water got really rough," he said, "and the boat was rocking up and down. I told her to stay down, but she kept saying she could help. The next thing I knew she stood up just as the boom came around. I watched as it hit her and threw her into the water. I was calling her name. I jumped in the water but could not find her." Matt raised his head with tears streaming down his face. "The hit from the boom must have knocked her out but a strap on her life vest had gotten caught on some rigging and forced her to stay face down in the water. She was only ten years old," he cried. "Why did it have to be Lisa? I'm so sorry, so sorry. But I don't even have the courage to ask God to heal my pain. I deserve to be miserable."

3. If you were in Matt's grief group, what would you say to him? What might you say to yourself to allow you to approach God's tender mercy?

_____

_____

_____

_____

_____

_____

"My aunt keeps telling me I'm being too hard on myself. I keep blaming myself that our baby died in his sleep. So I get what Matt is saying. But here's the part I don't get. Why did God give us this baby just to have him die? Makes no sense. One day I ran into a friend of ours who is a pediatrician. He explained a lot to me about SIDS. There wasn't anything I could have done. My aunt was right. I was being too hard on myself. One day at church my husband and I prayed for God's mercy. And it worked. We went home and looked at our other children and realized we were truly blessed. We have three great kids. It's just that one lives in heaven."

 Healing prayer for today: Come into my life, Lord Jesus. I invite you into my sorrow. Come.

Can I Invite God into My Sorrow?

Submit yourselves therefore to God. Resist the devil,
and he will flee from you. Draw near to God, and he
will draw near to you.

—James 4:7–8a

Our Lord is a gentleman. He will not go where he is not wanted or not welcome. He does not intrude, but gently stands by, waiting to be invited into our lives.

Chip, a man who faced the death of his wife and two children, said, "I don't know how you go through something like this without God. How do you do that? I can't even imagine getting through a day without the help of the Lord. Without him, I would have thrown in the towel."

"I wish I had your faith, but I just don't," said Pauleen. "I guess I lost it along the way." Pauleen was there on September 11. She worked in the building but was late for work. "I heard the explosion and ducked into an alleyway. I stopped and looked up and saw many of my coworkers jumping from the building. I just stood there and watched them hit the pavement. I can't get that sound out of my head. I blamed God for a long time. I yelled at him, I cursed him. I blamed him for it all. I hardly think I can ask God for help after that."

The Good News is that you can. Inviting God into your sorrow takes so little effort. All you have to do is ask. Even if you don't know him very well, or if you have not been formally introduced, you can invite this guest into your life with a simple invitation: Come.

1. Are you new to faith? Have you always had faith? Have you invited God into your pain? What do you think might happen if you did?

_____

_____

_____

_____

_____

_____

_____

Sitting at a stoplight, George glanced at the bumper sticker on the car in front of him. It read: "Joy is not the absence of sorrow but the presence of God." The familiar black pain started to engulf him again. He pulled into the Home Depot parking lot, shaking. He had not known anything but sorrow since the night of the phone call fourteen months earlier. "The caller identified himself as a policeman in the town about fifteen miles away, the town where my son lived with his girlfriend. She had been out with some girlfriends that evening. She came home and discovered Dennis was dead. He was naked, hanging in a closet by a belt."

"I didn't understand, Dennis had no reason to commit suicide. He had just gotten out of college, had a great job and a terrific girlfriend. I couldn't make sense of it. My wife and I kept blaming ourselves. What had we done wrong? I prayed God would help me understand. I hadn't read the coroner's report that was sent to us, but something made me finally open the envelope. Cause of death: 'Erotic asphyxiation.' What the hell was that? I didn't even know what it was. I had to look it up on the internet. Evidently it is a practice of cutting off a person's air intake to achieve a sexual high. At first I was shocked. But what helped was the article said that usually the person has no intention of committing suicide. I didn't know this either, but the accidental death rate with this thing is very high. So, God did answer our prayer as to why, and also gave us relief that Dennis didn't hang himself. Did it stop our grieving, no, but it helped."

2. If Jesus sat down next to you, what might you ask him? How might you ask him to come into your sorrow?

_____

_____

_____

_____

_____

"I can't take this Lord! That's what I'd tell him. I'd ask him to put his arms around me, give me a hug, and then fix everything so I could be happy again," says Debbie. "Will I ever be happy again? I don't know. I'd like to hope so. And with Jesus, there is hope. So I pray. And all I can say to him, is, help me, Lord."

3. If you have already asked God to share your sorrows, in what way have you seen or felt his presence?

_____

_____

_____

_____

_____

"My daughter Najwa and her family were killed in Lebanon," says Leyla. "A terrorist bomb hit their house directly, killing them all. Najwa had just had a baby, a little girl named Azar. I was planning to go see the baby, but they were killed before I could go. Azar was only a month old and I never got to see her. I prayed to God, if I could only have seen her face! I'd go to bed each night with the prayer on my lips. Maybe in a dream, I'll see her. A week or so after I prayed, a letter arrived. Inside the letter was a photo of my granddaughter, Azar. Azar in Lebanese means scarlet. She was wearing a red dress. Her face was exactly like my daughter's. So, God answered my prayer. I saw her face."

 Healing prayer for today: Come into my life, Lord Jesus. I invite you into my sorrow.

The Relationship Continues

He answered, "You shall love the Lord your God
with all your heart, and with all your soul, and with
all your strength, and with all your mind; and your
neighbor as yourself." And he said to him, "You have
given the right answer; do this, and you will live."
—Luke 10:27–28

While crossing a busy street, Sandy's nine-year-old son was killed by a car. "I was his mother but what am I now? I mean if your husband dies, you're called a widow. But if your child dies, what are you? There's no word to describe what you are."

Yes there is: "Mother"

Sandy is still Brian's mother. As Leslie, a woman whose son James was stillborn, explains, "I look at myself as a non-custodial parent. My son lives, but not here. He lives with his heavenly Father."

Sandy and Leslie will be mothers until the day they die. As with all of us whose loved ones have gone on, the relationship and love we once shared is not over, just changed. We are still connected with our loved ones in our thought, prayer, and love. That love will never leave. Take comfort in knowing that they, too, carry on that precious relationship.

"I love Communion even more these days," says Sandy, "because when I receive the bread and wine, I think of Brian receiving at the same time with all the company of heaven. During that moment I feel closest to my son and that gives me great comfort."

Physically, our loved ones are gone, but their souls live on with Christ. We will always be connected with them through our Lord Jesus. Because we are both connected to him, we are there in communion forever.

"When my mother died, I realized I was now the matriarch of our family. I really did not want this position. I don't care if I do have kids of my own; I always knew my mom was there. However, I soon realized there were so many ways my relationship with my mom was not dead, just changed. Now whenever I honor her legacy by continuing her traditions, I feel her presence. I continue to celebrate holidays in her habits. The Fourth of July is next week and I have already made out my list: watermelon-eating contest for the kids, apple pie with Mom's famous caramel sauce, sparklers, and last but not least, Grandpa's 'patriotic punch!' I can feel my mom smiling over my shoulder. And I feel close to her again."

1. How is your relationship with your loved one continuing? Where are some of the places you go or things you do that make you feel his or her presence?

_____

_____

_____

_____

_____

_____

"My dad was a woodworker and he was really good. He made a cradle for me when I was a baby. When we found out we were going to have a girl, I started to make a cradle. I mean, how hard could it be, right?" laughs Jacob. "Oh boy, was I wrong! I wanted to give up, but I kept hearing my dad's voice in the back of my head saying, 'You can do this. Our family are not quitters.' And the whole time I was sanding and painting, I felt close to him. I was continuing his work."

2. How are you sharing this person's legacy?

_____

_____

_____

_____

"We are Polish and for big religious events my grandmother always made a lamb cake. I had forgotten about that until a cousin was having a Christening for her new baby. I said I would bring a lamb cake. I had my grandmother's mold and her recipe, so I baked it. Well, the dang head fell off! I was devastated. I called my mom in tears. 'Oh, that always happened to Babcia. Put a Popsicle stick in its neck.' I took the cake to the church and put it on the table. The head started to list. My mom was next to me and said, 'Yeah that always happened too.' I cracked up."

 Healing prayer for today: Lord, God, you loved us so much you gladly sacrificed your only son so that we may have eternal life. For that I thank you. Thank you, too, for that heavenly reunion you have planned when I will see my loved one again.

Is There Really a Heaven? Will I See My Loved One Again?

But now that you have been freed from sin and enslaved to God, the advantage you get is sanctification. The end is eternal life. For the wages of sin is death, but the free gift of God is eternal life in Christ Jesus our Lord.
—ROMANS 6:22–23

If there is no eternal life, then there was no reason for Jesus to come. If there is no eternal life, there would have been no reason for Jesus to die. If there is no eternal life, Jesus would not have risen from the dead. He did. We will.

Our longing for a heavenly reunion is an affirmation that heaven exists. If it were not so, we would not keep wanting, waiting, and wondering which day our reunion will come.

Heaven is real. Jesus is real. His love for us, and his longing that we will one day be with him and all the company of heaven, is also real. And here's the best part: You don't have to do anything to earn eternal life. It's a free gift already given to all believers. "But it has now been revealed through the appearing of our Savior Christ Jesus, who abolished death and brought life and immortality to light through the gospel" (2 Timothy 1:10).

All those who believe in Christ will see their loved ones again. What you do while waiting for that reunion gives you much to talk about.

1. Has there been moment when you doubted the existence of heaven?

_____

_____

_____

_____

_____

_____

_____

Patsy was tired. Since the freak death of her husband in a rock climbing accident, she had not been able to sleep well. Her head kept spinning. She had so many questions, so many 'what ifs.' The question in her head was, "Is heaven real?" She thought of all the times she had joked that her heavenly body was going to be tall, thin, and blonde. But was it real?

"I couldn't sleep. I looked at the clock on my bedside table as it flipped to 3:00. I immediately thought, 'Wait, Jesus can't lie.' I sat up and repeated, 'Jesus can't lie.' Somewhere in one of the Gospels Jesus says something about going to prepare a place for us and if it was not so he would not have said it. And Jesus can't lie!"

2. When you are reunited in heaven, what things would you want to say to your loved one?

_____

_____

_____

_____

_____

_____

"My Aunt and I were very close," says Alyssa. "After my parents died, she pretty much raised me. So when she died I took it hard. We weren't church-going people. Just Christmas and Easter. We really never talked about faith. I didn't really learn about Jesus until I got to college. So when she died, I worried that my sweet aunt wasn't a real believer. That she didn't get into heaven. When we were getting ready for the estate sale, I found her bible. She had so many things underlined and written in the margins. I read some of the things she had written and then I knew. She knew Jesus. And as a believer, she's in heaven. I so want to tell her how happy I am about that."

"I want to know where my wife hid the dang bottle opener!" laughs Dick. "I can't find it anywhere. It was old and a bit rusty, but it was my favorite. I'm a big Green Bay Packers fan and it had their logo on it. I used it all the time. I think she must have thrown it out. Are you allowed to fuss at your wife in heaven?"

3. What are some things you have done since your loved one has died that you look forward to telling them about?

_____

_____

_____

_____

_____

_____

_____

Karl takes a big breath and says, "Both my parents died in a car accident a couple of years ago. I had to drop out of college my senior year to take care of my little brother. I can't wait to tell them that I finished school at night and that John is now a freshman."

4. Describe what you think heaven will look like.

_____

_____

_____

_____

_____

_____

_____

"Know there will be no sorrow. I'm looking forward to that," said Laney. "I do hope we can be reunited with our loved ones. I have to count on God's grace for that, because my father was not a believer. A good man, but not a believer."

Jack says, "My wife and I used to talk about what heaven looks like. When I look around the world and see such wonders of nature, I cannot even begin to comprehend what heaven will be like. To be better than this? Wow. It's going to be pretty amazing."

 Healing prayer for today: Lord, how I long to see my loved one again! I thank you for preparing a place for us in your heavenly kingdom. While I must remain here, and my loved one remains with you, help me to find a new purpose for the life I have still to live. Fill my life, Lord Jesus, with your love and presence.

Death Is Not the End of Our Relationship

The last enemy to be destroyed is death.
—1 CORINTHIANS 15:26

It may be interesting to know that the Hebrew word for "breath" and "soul" are the same. Judaic Midrash or folktale teaches that at each person's birth, God himself breathes a soul into the body. God only loans this soul to us and it must be returned to him. Such is death.

But death is not an end. It is the beginning. Saint Paul tells us, "Yes, we do have confidence, and we would rather be away from the body and at home with the Lord" (2 Corinthians 5:8). How can we be sure that what Paul says is true? The proof lies in the fact that Jesus came back to us after his death. How do we know that he actually came back? Because there were hundreds of witnesses who saw him.

Jesus abolished death forever, not just for himself, but also for you. "I will not leave you orphaned; I am coming to you. In a little while the world will no longer see me, but you will see me; because I live, you also will live (John 14:18–19). As Pasty said, "Jesus can't lie." Jesus is incapable of telling a lie, it's not in his character. So we must believe that what he says is an absolute truth. Death is temporary.

When we leave this world, life is not over. Your loved one lives again. They have gone to be with our Lord with all those believers who have gone on before them. While you continue to love them in this world, they continue to love you in the next. Their life goes on, as will yours, a little more joyfully each day.

1. When you hear that your loved ones in heaven continue to love you even now, what does that bring to mind?

_____

_____

_____

_____

_____

_____

Norma's denomination teaches that the dead are not really dead, but merely sleeping. That idea tormented her for months. "I kept thinking, is my Mom scared? Is she cold in that grave? Can she breathe? I would go to her grave and yell, 'Momma can you hear me?' I went to talk to another minister in a different denomination. I wanted to hear what she thought about it. That's when she reminded me that Jesus told the guy on the cross next to him, 'Today you will be with me in paradise.' Today. I can't begin to tell you how relieved I felt. She's not in that cold grave but in paradise. And she still loves me! And she is not cold or scared but happy."

2. Sometimes knowing that the relationship continues through love can be confusing. Especially for those who had been married. What does it mean to you, that your relationship continues in a heavenly manner?

_____

_____

_____

_____

_____

_____

Diego decided to go out more. "Maria, my wife of twenty years, has been dead for two years. We battled the cancer for three years before that." He rubbed his eyes with his hands and said, "I really can't believe the time that has gone by. I have done everything they told me to do— took the cruise, read the books, and attended the family support groups." He went on to say, "At best, the last two years have been confusing and frustrating. The loneliness has been overwhelming." He continued to share that he had always been a faithful husband, but now he craved the intimacy he once shared with Maria. But he felt a sense of guilt. Was he being unfaithful to even think about loving another woman?

"I met Julia six months ago at a neighborhood cookout. Two months ago we got engaged." He related that his two daughters were furious with him. He said he remembered fingering the ring on his wedding day wondering if he was doing the right thing. Fr. Juan Cruz at the Catholic church where he and Julia had been attending was going to perform the wedding. "Elena, my eldest, refused to come to the service, and Christina, her younger sister, was there but making it abundantly clear it was under protest."

Diego shared that he knew in his heart that his relationship with Maria would never be fully ended. She was and always would be woven into the fabric of his life, but now it was time to "weave a new life" with Julia. As much as he loved Julia, he still had some guilt knowing his daughters didn't approve of his marriage, even though his church seemed delighted and was very supportive. Also, he worried if God approved. So he went to see his priest.

"Fr. Cruz had introduced me to 'Miss Anna,' an older, longtime member of the church. When she learned about Maria's death and my remarriage, Miss Anna looked me in the face and said, 'I understand. My husband Luis left me for another man sixteen years ago.'" His grief group giggled as Diego continued, admitting he had had the same reaction. "Miss Anna went on to say, 'Yes, Luis left me to be with Jesus. He will always live in my heart, but I knew I had to go on. I was not dead. I had to live again.'" Diego said, "I knew in that moment God was speaking to me through this dear lady."

Diego said he knew the relationship with Maria would never end, but like Miss Anna said, "It was time to go and live again."

3. Is there anything that might be preventing you from "living again"?

_____

_____

_____

_____

_____

_____

_____

"My mother was a very judgmental woman. With her it was always black or white, which is kind of funny to say because she was very racist," laughs Roger. "I never told my mother that I was gay but I think she suspected it. I never brought my boyfriend around because I knew she wouldn't approve. I knew she wouldn't understand. And Tony's black. She definitely would not have approved of that! So I lived my life in secret. But after she died, Tony and I got married. For the first time in my life I am truly happy. I love my mother, always will, but the woman was a bigot."

 Healing prayer for today: Precious Lord, keep my loved one safe in your loving presence. Help me to get through this grief by remembering that death is only temporary and that my loved one lives again with you.

I'm Afraid I Will Forget My Loved One

They shall celebrate the fame of your abundant
goodness, and shall sing aloud of your righteousness.
—Psalm 145:7

I can't remember my father's face," cried Anne. "I can barely remember his voice. I'm forgetting him, and that makes me so sad. What if I forget him completely?"

Anne will never forget her father. Perhaps the picture of his face will become fuzzy, but it will never be totally blurred and neither will her memories, which bring him once more into focus. During the initial months of grief, you can't think clearly. Your memory of most things is temporarily blocked. Temporarily.

Often there can be a fear that if you stop grieving, you might stop remembering. By moving on, do you fear you are leaving your loved one behind? Impossible. You have loved them, cared for them, shared your life with them.

As your grief walk continues, and your healing continues, so will your recollections. As your memory returns, so will the details of your loved ones. Your lives are forever intertwined in an intricate life tapestry. While some of the fringes may fray for a while, in time the memory that binds the two of you will return. Will you ever forget your loved ones? Never!

"Our twelve-year-old son woke us up in the middle of the night crying. When he finally calmed enough, he blurted out, 'I can't remember what Granddaddy looked like.' His words tore my heart out because I, too, was beginning to find it difficult to perfectly picture my dad's face," says Adelaide. "I felt a little stab of guilt wondering if I was forgetting Dad. I told myself I was imagining things. I knew I would never forget him. I can somehow picture my dad's kind eyes and shaking his head in that particular way. He knows I will never forget him but he also does not want me to forget to live my life. As I was putting my son back to bed, just before he closed his eyes I realized he had the same piercing blue eyes of my father and I thought to myself, 'Oh no, I will never forget.' Thank you God for those blue eyes."

1. Do you fear that you might forget? Have you experienced the worry of forgetting? What helped you to remember?

_____

_____

_____

_____

_____

_____

"I have no photos of any of my great grandparents or any of my older relatives," says Lilly. "They were killed in the Holocaust. You know it wasn't just Jews that were murdered but Christians, too. All my great uncles and aunts, great grandparents. I won't forget what happened to them, but how can I remember someone I haven't met? One day my daughter had to do a family tree for school with photos. She was very upset that we had no pictures. I suggested she find pictures in a magazine of what she thought they might look like. When she was finished I felt in a strange way that I finally met them!"

2. What are the three things you most want to remember about your loved one?

_____

_____

_____

_____

_____

_____

"My sister Beth was only two when our dad died; a heart attack at the age of forty-two," says Mignon. "She asked me what Dad was like, to tell her stories, but I didn't have very many. I was only sixteen when he died, so I asked my aunt and grandparents about him. I remembered so many things after that. I also got his military records. I had no idea of the things he did. He was a war hero, won two Silver Stars, and I didn't know anything about that. I want to remember that he was a hero, a daddy who played with us, and that he was very funny. My aunt says I am a lot like him because he really loved life and all the people in it. I guess I am like that. I've really never met a stranger."

"I want to remember my mom's golden eyes. They really were amber-colored. We used to tease her and she'd waltz around the room, batting her eyes to us and saying, 'You're so jealous.' I didn't notice for a very long time that my grandson has those same colored eyes. She would have been so proud."

"Binh was only ten when he died. I have lots of photos of him all over the house, but what I don't want to forget," says Chau, "is the way he always saw the invisible people on the streets. If there was a person in a wheelchair, he'd always stop and say hello. Or a panhandler, or a police officer, or someone sitting all alone on a bench. I try now to do the same and that makes me remember what a kind child Binh was."

 Healing prayer for today: Dear Lord, I place my fear that I may forget precious details of my loved one into your gentle hands. Restore my memory, Lord. Help me to have clear vision of them once more.

DAY 24

Will I Ever Be Able to Get Over My Grief?

The saying is sure and worthy of full acceptance.
For to this end we toil and struggle, because we have
our hope set on the living God, who is the Savior of
all people, especially of those who believe.
—1 TIMOTHY 4:9–10

Do you still wake up early in the morning, wondering if the death of your loved one was just a bad dream? That's not uncommon. Do you often think you see a loved one in a crowded room or walking down a street? That's not unusual.

There is no rulebook for grief. No schedule, no code of conduct. We just go through it at our own pace, in our own time, and in our own unique way. Acceptance will come.

Ignoring or denying your grief, however, will not make the pain go away. Grief is sort of like a skinned knee. If you don't seek first aid, the wound will fester and never heal. How long does it take to heal grief? As long as it takes.

While there is no right or wrong way to grieve (unless you are doing something harmful in the process), there are things that can help you adjust to life without your loved one. Sharing with friends who also suffer grief, or joining a bereavement group, or discussing your grief with a member of the clergy allows you the opportunity to talk about your loved one.

Can't find any of these? Then talk to your Lord, "Be merciful to me, O God, be merciful to me, for in you my soul takes refuge; in the shadow of your wings I will take refuge, until the destroying storms pass by" (Psalm 57:1). He's the greatest listener and our Jesus will send you comfort. Each conversation you have about your loved one is a giant step forward toward recovery, and you will begin to heal.

No, you will never fully "get over" your grief. You will miss your loved one the rest of your life. But the sorrow of grief that you feel now does fade. The intense pain you are feeling now will begin to diminish. It just might not happen today.

1. While you never "get over" grief, describe how you are getting through it today.

"Our friends, Joyce and Mark, insisted we attend a grief conference at the church. It was the last thing I wanted to do, but my husband is starting to worry that I am in an irreversible downward spiral," says Addie. "My ex-husband, who is a mean drunk on the best of days, ran over my son in the driveway. I had promised myself I would never leave John alone with his father again, but John was a teenager and I was trying not to hover. I started off the porch when my ex-husband yelled, 'Move it kid. I'm in a hurry.' Everything went into slow motion. John was getting something out of the trunk. He must not have heard his father who suddenly threw the car into reverse. I will never forget the sound. The car stopped but not before my beautiful boy lay in our driveway, bleeding, broken, and dying. All I remember is screaming and screaming. When my son was a little boy, he loved Buzz Lightyear. It has been almost three years since that day and I still cannot sleep without that Buzz Lightyear doll. I don't know if I will ever be able to get over it. The reality is, as a wise friend once shared, 'You don't get over grief, you get through it.'"

"I wear my uncle's jacket," says Esther. "I can still smell him. I know its plaid and it doesn't go with anything I own, but I wear it nearly every day. I look like an idiot, but I just don't care. I wear that jacket. My mom's worried I will wear it on my wedding day. Well," she laughs, "I just might."

2. What are you doing to actively work through your grief?

_____

_____

_____

_____

_____

_____

_____

"My husband died about a year ago. My sister mentioned his name and I lost it. She says to me, 'Good grief, Sadie, it's been a year already. Shouldn't you be over this by now?' I got right into her face and said, 'It's _only_ been a year!' I'm doing the best I know how to. And I'm giving myself permission to cry any ole time I want to. And as long as I want to."

Julie is very quiet and squirms around in her seat before she says, "My minister made things worse. I tried to go see him for some pastoral counseling. Know what he told me? If I really had faith, I would be happy that my son is in heaven with Jesus. I was furious. What a dumb thing to tell a mother in grief. I stood up from my chair and said, 'Well Pastor, you go ahead and be happy that Charlie is happy in heaven. He's not here. I can't hug him, or talk with him or kiss his face!' Then I stormed out. I'm glad I found a good grief group. And a new pastor."

3. Well-intentioned people often say platitudes that are not helpful. Have you experienced that?

_____

_____

_____

_____

_____

_____

"Oh yeah," says Grace. "When I was in the hospital after I lost the baby, this nurse says to me, 'Well honey, you can always have another baby.' Really? That's what you say to a woman whose baby just died? I'll never have THIS baby, lady. And for the record, I did not have a miscarriage. I had a baby that died."

"At the reception after the funeral of my step-father, this woman comes up to my mother and says, 'Now, sweetie, don't you be sad that he's gone. He wasn't that nice a man anyway. He even made a pass at me one day.' At the funeral reception for crying out loud. Oh, yeah, that was comforting to my mother."

 Healing prayer for today: Merciful Father, have pity on me. Deliver me from this sorrow and restore me to joy. Help me see your world as a wondrous place once more.

I Know I'm Starting to Heal When...

He himself bore our sins in his body on the cross, so that, free from sins, we might live for righteousness; by his wounds you have been healed.
 —1 PETER 2:24

What are the signs that you are beginning to heal?

"I knew I was starting to get better when I finally slept through the night," said Kiersten.

"The day I could box up my wife's clothes and actually give them away was a huge step," said Dan.

"When I could watch the other children in the neighborhood play and not get angry that they live and my daughter doesn't," said Doris.

The signs of recovery, or healing, can be so subtle we may not even notice them at first. But they're there. Sleeping through the night. Having a day without tears. Going to a party and actually finding yourself having fun. Talking about your loved one and laughing at old stories instead of crying. No longer having that sense of complete physical exhaustion. Going back to work, meeting new friends, finding new things to do with your life. These are affirmations of healing and they will come.

You may not be at this place right now, but you will be. There will come a day when you stop crying. There will come a time when you sleep through the night. And there will come a day when you look forward to things in life, even though your loved one will not be a part of them. Look for these signs. Hope for these signs. Pray they will come. These victories signify that you will always remember your loved one, and by fully living again, you honor their memory with joy instead of sorrow.

1. Name at least one victory that you have experienced during your grief.

_____

_____

_____

_____

_____

_____

_____

Mona pulled into the drive-thru line at Starbucks. She ordered a tall pumpkin spiced latte that was the special in October. She drove away, turned right at the stoplight, and headed to the hospital. "Here I am having a pumpkin latte and my niece who is only twenty-two is dying. How can this be?"

Ultimately her niece, who was really more like a daughter to her, did die. Mona could not go anywhere near a Starbucks. The holidays came and went and she could not stand the thought of pumpkin pie, pumpkin bread, or _anything_ pumpkin. "The first-year anniversary rolled around and I smelled a pumpkin spiced candle in a gift shop. It made me so ill I ran out of the store. I would see pumpkins in the grocery store and wanted to smash them all."

Another year passed. Mona was on her way to a meeting and decided to get a coffee on the way. She pulled into Starbucks without thinking. As she started to order she noticed that the spiced pumpkin lattes were back for a limited time. Suddenly, she smiled and into the garbled microphone she boldly ordered a tall pumpkin spice latte. "As I sipped my coffee I started to smile. Yes, I'm always going to miss my niece, but there are so many wonderful things to remember. I smiled because it was then that I remembered that I used to call my niece my little pumpkin. That's also when I realized my healing had begun."

"I went to the military funeral of a friend. I wasn't sure I could do it. My father was buried at Arlington and had a military funeral," Marsha said. "But I promised Tom I would go. I did okay through Taps, but when the Missing Man Plane formation started, I had a real lump in my throat. I didn't bawl like I did with my dad's, just a lump. I think that's real progress."

2. Sometimes it's hard returning to a place that you once shared. Have you been able to do that? If so, where did you go and what was it like?

_____

_____

_____

_____

_____

_____

_____

"I went to the Christmas parade in our little town. I used to take my granddaughter every year," says Chuck. "I just couldn't go last year, but I did this year. And it was okay. I didn't cry. I actually enjoyed watching the neighborhood kids who were in the parade. I miss Carla, I really do. I think going to the parade actually helped me because it had always been our special time together."

"I went back to the place where Ted died. It had been a scuba diving accident in Bermuda. I felt compelled to go back. I put on my tanks and gear and swam to the cave where he had died. I didn't go in, but I placed some flowers at the entrance. I forgot to weigh them down, so immediately they floated up. And that was okay. It was as if they were floating up to heaven where Ted is. It was kind of sweet. Then I went to the Swizzle Inn where we used to hang out. I saw some of his friends and we had a rum Swizzle in his honor. It was a great day, the kind of day Ted would have loved."

 Healing prayer for today: Thank you, Jesus, for the healing you have begun in me. I give you praise and glory that you are rescuing me from my distress and restoring my soul.

I Feel So Hopeless

But this I call to mind, and therefore I have hope:
The steadfast love of the Lord never ceases, his
mercies never come to an end; they are new every
morning; great is your faithfulness. "The Lord is
my portion," says my soul, "therefore I will hope
in him."

—Lamentations 3:21–24

When you are in the middle of pain, and you feel as if everything that ever mattered to you and gave your life meaning is gone, hope that life will be joyful again seems elusive and even, at times, impossible.

"It feels so bad, this grief thing. I was married to Tim right out of high school. All my memories are tied up with him," says Karen, whose entire family was killed in a car wreck. "He and our boys were my whole life. Now that they're gone, I'm totally lost. I don't know why I lived and they didn't but I have to believe there is a reason."

For Karen to believe that there is some reason why she is to go on living, while the rest of her family is dead, affirms that God in his mercy has given Karen an expectation that her life can be full again. He has given her hope. He will give her purpose.

You may be feeling numb with pain. That's to be expected. Yet while things might seem discouraging, your life is not without hope because your hope is with the Lord.

1. What is it that you hope for? What might be keeping you from embracing hope for a new and joy-filled life?

_____

_____

_____

_____

_____

_____

_____

"I guess I feel unworthy of his hope. It takes all the strength I have just to wake up in the morning. I can't believe the things I had to do to survive," says Tonya, who waded through the waters after Katrina to get to safety. "I had to walk past floating bodies of those who didn't make it. I can't begin to tell you the horror of what I saw. I consider myself a good Christian, but I did things I'm not proud of that day just to survive."

Two weeks had passed since Tonya had been rescued from the flooded area of the city of New Orleans. The horror of that event brings her such remorse, grief, and guilt.

"I'm grieving for my friends and neighbors who didn't make it. Why them? Why not me? I was one of the fortunate ones. I survived. Talk about walking through the valley of the shadow of death, I did that. I walked past many dead bodies. I pushed them out of the way like trash and kept going. I'm alive, but I have such guilt about being alive. My house is gone. Everything in the house is gone. The only hope I have to restart my life is to hope that Jesus will forgive me and help me. I have nowhere else to turn."

2. Describe the first time you felt that there was hope that you would get through this.

_____

_____

_____

_____

_____

_____

_____

Dean's son and daughter had been killed in a car accident while coming back from college. Six months later his wife died suddenly of pancreatic cancer.

"My life was full. I had all kinds of hope that our kids would finish college, get married, and my wife and I would retire and spend our time with grandkids. Then all of a sudden, I'm completely alone. Until I met Gina. She gave me hope. She had three kids, also in college, when her husband was killed in a burglary at his store. It had been two years for each of us. When we got married, I became a stepfather to her kids. It was wonderful. Her daughter is getting married in June. My hope is that she and her husband have a boat-load of kids. That's my new hope, to become a grandfather. God answered my prayers for a new life. I couldn't have made it through all this if I didn't have faith that God had a plan for me."

3. Even in your deepest grief, can you imagine that God has a plan for you? A new life filled with abundant joy?

_____

_____

_____

_____

_____

_____

"I'm getting there," says Joyce. "Susan was my best friend. We met in basic training. We got through it together. When I received orders to deploy to Afghanistan, so did Susan. In fact, we were on the same plane. We talked a lot about what we would do after the Army. Both of us planned to go to college together. We talked about how we would be each other's maid of honor when we got married. That we'd live near each other and raise our kids together. We talked about all the things we'd do when we got back. But she was killed driving over a land mine. I'm getting married in a few months. Susan won't be there. That hurts. I know I'll find joy in the life Rob and I will have. He's a wonderful man. An Army officer. But I will miss Susan probably for the rest of my life."

"I slammed the sympathy card down on the countertop and wished I could punch something," Marcus almost shouted. "One more sticky sweet card talking about hope. What is hope anyway?" he asked. "Because right now, I certainly do not have any."

Patrice was his life; his confidante, his lover, and his best friend. They had met through friends and had moved in together. They had a great life, traveling to all their bucket list places. That is, until she was diagnosed with cancer.

"Some of my friends have said six months is long enough to grieve and now I need to snap out of it and get back out there," he stated. "My only thoughts are, 'Why and what for?' Patrice is gone so what is the use of going out?" he asked. "I'll never find another Patrice. And I don't want to."

Marcus stopped for a long while, but you could still sense he had more to say. Finally, he said in a flat voice, "I don't even know if I want to live, let alone go out. Hope? What is that?"

 Healing prayer for today: Lord Jesus, I ask you to grant me the gift of your hope. Deliver me from despair, and instead fill my life with anticipation and joy.

DAY 27

Thanking God for His Tender Mercies

I thank my God every time I remember you.
   —PHILIPPIANS 1:3

In time of sorrow, sometimes it's hard to thank God for his tender mercies. But they are there nonetheless. You just have to look for them.

"I remember a very difficult night when my dear mother-in-law, Sarah, was in great pain. I could find nothing to soothe her. Then a compassionate nurse came in with a tape recorder and some wonderful hymns. Listening to that glorious music, Sarah was able to find solace and comfort during those last moments of life. I will be forever grateful to our Lord for sending that very special nurse to us."

1. There are moments during the last few months of your grief when God has sent you helpmates to get through your days. Have you thanked him?

_____

_____

_____

_____

_____

_____

_____

"I wouldn't say Bette was a friend of mine, just someone I knew from church. In fact, I often avoided her because she talks all the time and drives me crazy. But one day she shows up at my door with dinner. She didn't stay, she didn't babble on like she usually does, she just gave me a hug and left. That was exactly what I needed that day. And I thanked God for her tender heart. That act of mercy has now made us friends."

2. God's presence is all around us. Sometimes we just don't notice. Did you thank him for the wonderful sunrise? For friends who came to comfort you in his name? For a clergy member who helped you get through the funeral? Maybe even for a neighbor who sent you a casserole. All these are tender mercies sent to you from your Lord. There will be more. And someday he will send you as a comfort to others.

_____

_____

_____

_____

_____

_____

Mateo leaned back in his chair and began by saying, "It has been the craziest week. I mean the wildest thing happened last Tuesday."

Mateo works for a travel group that specializes in cutting-edge, adventure-style trips. "It was last week's staff meeting. We were talking about adding a new line of sailing trips to our vacation offerings. I looked over at Pamela and she was frozen, like she could not breathe," he said. He explained to the group that Pamela's son, Devin, had died in a catamaran accident about four months before.

"I don't know what came over me but I knew exactly what was happening to her because it had happened to me when my brother died," Mateo said. "My brother died in a skiing accident. The first time someone started talking about a ski vacation, I was paralyzed with grief. I remember feeling like I was drowning but without water."

Mateo said that he had come up with a "lame but plausible" excuse to leave the meeting and asked if Pamela could come help him. He shared that after they had gotten to the hallway away from the meeting room, Pamela had started to shake uncontrollably. "When will it stop, will it ever stop?" Pamela had asked Mateo. "I told her in a while but for right now, it is awful. But I am here for you. I would not ever have thought I could have done anything like that. It is totally not me, but I think my brother would be proud."

3. As hard as grief is, and it truly is, there are tender moments. Moments for which we forgot to thank God. What are some of those sweet moments for you?

_____

_____

_____

_____

_____

_____

"Our neighbor is a Greek lady," says Liam. "She knows how much I love moussaka and how much my dad loved it. I tried making it once for him, but it's a lot of work. But she took the time to make it and bring it to my wife and me. She called it Greek comfort food, and it was. When I returned the dish to her, she sat me down, gave me a small glass of ouzo, and said we were going to toast my dad for the life he lived. I didn't have the heart to tell her I don't like ouzo, but that gesture meant the world to me."

Jane's daughter was only eight when she was killed in a car accident. "The church school wanted to do a memorial service for her. The kids in her class were having a rough time dealing with Carrie's death. At the end of the service we went outside and each of the children had a balloon with a message for Carrie attached to it. The pastor prayed and then the children let go of the balloons. We all watched as the messages floated toward heaven. One little boy said to me, 'Don't worry. When Carrie gets our messages she will be happy.' That was the sweetest thing anyone could have done for us."

Robert seemed lost in thought as he began to speak. "At the time I could not see God's mercy. All I could see was my beloved wife, machines, doctors and nurses conferring, and finally someone offering me a clip-board and asking for my signature to unhook her from the ventilator. There really was no decision, per se, to be made. Just an acceptance of cold hard fact, that this was the end." Robert paused and then contin-ued, "Two friends were there with me. It was Sunday morning and one had just come from church. She had brought cards that all our church friends had signed with love and blessings. She began to read the cards, and my dear wife slipped peacefully away through the words of love and prayers from others." As he wiped away the tears from his eyes Rob-ert said, "Looking back, I can't imagine anything more tender or God-orchestrated. I will always be grateful for that moment."

 Healing prayer for today: Lord, I often forget to thank you for all the things you do for me. Forgive me. For all your tender mercies, I give you glory and praise, and I thank you, Lord, that you never forget me.

Remembering
Our Loved One

Come to him, a living stone, though rejected by
mortals yet chosen and precious in God's sight,
and like living stones, let yourselves be built
into a spiritual house, to be a holy priesthood,
to offer spiritual sacrifices acceptable to God
through Jesus Christ.
    —1 PETER 2:4–5

In Jerusalem during the time of King Solomon, there was a separate
path around the Jewish Temple for mourners to walk. As others in the
community noticed those in grief, they offered solace by saying, "May
God comfort you among the mourners of Zion and Jerusalem." Though
the Temple is gone, our Jewish friends take part in a ritual of mourning
that is called a mourner's path. When the year is over, a tombstone is
placed at the gravesite for the first time. Visitors place a small stone on
the grave to remind themselves that while they remember and miss their
loved one, they must remain here in this life, while their loved one must
remain with God.

We are of different worlds now, our deceased loved ones and we who
still live. The love that we have for each other in Christ brings deep sorrow when we are parted by death. But this separation is not forever, for
"neither death, nor life, nor angels, nor rulers, nor things present, nor
things to come nor height, nor depth, nor anything else in all creation,
will be able to separate us from the love of God in Christ Jesus our Lord"
(Romans 8:38–39).

The stone placed on a Christian grave is not a physical pebble. Ours
is the remembrance of our Lord himself, for he alone ransomed us from
the grave.

1. How have you felt the presence of your loved one, even though you know they are in heaven and not here?

_____

_____

_____

_____

_____

_____

"I had a wisteria bush that never bloomed. My mother's always did. Every spring she would ask me to come by her house, always with some kind of excuse. Then she'd show me her fully blooming wisteria and ask, 'How's your wisteria doing?' And then she would laugh like crazy. No matter what I did to that bush, it never would bloom. I went over to her house for the last time in the spring, right after I had sold it. Sure enough her bush was blooming like crazy. It made me smile. I went home to look at my bush, and there it was. One bloom. It never bloomed again, but I think God sent me that one blossom as a message that she is okay and is with him."

2. Have you felt God's comforting presence?

_____

_____

_____

_____

_____

_____

"For me it was Christmas Eve. Our baby had been the Christ child in the manger last year. He slept through the whole Nativity. Going to church to see another babe in the manger was going to be so hard. I prayed to God I would be able to get through it. I really dreaded it. The Nativity play started and the baby in the manger started to cry. Then he started to scream like crazy, nearly drowning out the rest of the children. Everyone began to laugh, including me, as the children screamed their lines as loud as they could. The louder the baby cried, the louder the children delivered their lines. In the middle of the play one of the little shepherds, who was dressed as a Dalmatian because he insisted on wearing his doggie costume, jumped up to the lectern and shouted, 'Come on cows, let's herd!' As the cows got up, the backdrop fell. When it was Mary's turn to say her line, she put her hands on her hips and yelled, 'His name is Jesus, for crying out loud!' It was the best nativity play ever. I needed to laugh and God allowed me to experience that."

Judy laughed, "I really believe this is one of my better ideas. The whole family is excited about it."

Judy's mom, Martha, loved birthdays and she always made everyone's birthday a huge, elaborate celebration. "Mom has been dead almost a year and a half now and her birthday is in a couple of months," Judy continued. "I'm going to give her a birthday party."

Judy outlined her plan. "I'm going to have a big family reunion and have a blowout birthday celebration in memory of Mom. I'm going to have custom tee-shirts made to say, 'Martha's Bunch.' In lieu of presents, everyone can chip in and make a donation to Habitat, my mom's favorite charity. And of course I'll make the coconut cake that was Mom's signature recipe," Judy laughs. "None of us like coconut, but we never told her."

As she finished, Judy sighed and said softly, "I know it will be a wonderful day of remembering Mom."

 Healing prayer for today: May God comfort me among the mourners of Zion and Jerusalem.

DAY 29

Standing Stones

I tell you, if these were silent,
the stones would shout out.
— Luke 19:40

The Old Testament is filled with stories of the patriarchs erecting Standing Stones. These stones marked events of importance so that travelers passing by would know something extraordinary happened there. Those who knew the stones' significance would tell the stories of how God had touched the lives of the ones who had erected the stones.

The Israelites' sacred monuments stood as a silent testimony to the presence and power of God. In the telling of the story about the circumstances causing the monuments to be built, listeners came to an awareness of God's power and love for his people.

Like the Israelites, you, too, have experienced a monumental event. Your loved one has died and you will never be the same again. How you choose to memorialize this event will be a testimony to the life of your loved one, the life you continue to live, and your relationship with God. You are now the witness to the life of your loved one—the Standing Stone that cries out, a living testimony to the power and love of God.

1. What Standing Stone have you done for your loved one?

_____

_____

_____

_____

_____

_____

"I remember watching the movie *Schindler's List.* At the end, people went to a graveyard and put stones on Schindler's grave to remember him. But my aunt and I decided to use cocktails instead," laughs Julia. "Every year I go to New Hampshire to the Polish cemetery to visit my mom's grave. We bring wine and give her a glass, like she's having happy hour with us." Julia starts to laugh harder. "Now at first that sounds like a good idea. Until one day when my aunt went to the grave without me and there was already a full glass of wine sitting there! She didn't put it there. She was convinced that my mother had returned from the dead! I found out later it was a good friend of hers who had been in town and had done the same thing. Scared the heck out of the little woman. My mom would have loved that."

"Our son, Brent, was killed at a Little League game when a bat was thrown and hit his head. The child who flung the bat took it as hard as we did. We worked with the boy's family, and together we raised money to buy safety helmets for all the teams in our city in the name of our son. I go to every game of my son's team and cheer for the boy who flung the bat. I think God used that boy to help me heal from Brent's death."

"My mother spray painted everything gold," said Cindy. Cindy bought her mother brass chargers. "She spray painted them gold. An old mirror? Gold. She was dangerous with a can of gold spray paint. The first Christmas she wasn't with us, in her honor, I spray painted an old wreath gold. You know what? It looked great!"

"I have been working on something for two years for my Aunt Lydia." Aunt Lydia had taken in Cynthia when her mom walked out on her. She had no clue who her father was and, frankly, doubted her mom knew either. But then there had been Aunt Lydia, and Cynthia loved her as a mother. "Aunt Lydia was an awesome gardener and could get anything to grow," Cynthia said. "I designed and planted an elaborate garden as a memory or Standing Stone to my aunt. It is so cool. It is so like Aunt Lydia: complex yet inviting, colorful and warm, very open but with intimate nooks with benches for quiet reflection."

Cynthia shared that whenever she was in the garden, alone or with friends and family, it reminded her of the blessing Aunt Lydia had been in her life. "She really helped me blossom. Now I watch flowers blossom."

 Healing prayer for today: Help me to live the rest of my life in a way that honors you and the memory of my loved one. Help me to be a Standing Stone of your love and faithfulness.

What Do I Do with the Rest of My Life?

Go forth into the world rejoicing in the power
of the Spirit.
—BOOK OF COMMON PRAYER

There are many soothing prayers in the Episcopal Book of Common Prayer. A prayer for those who mourn reads, "Grant to all who mourn a sure confidence in your Fatherly care, that, casting all their grief on you, they may know the consolation of your Love."

We find new meaning to our lives in the resurrection of Jesus. We know that because he died and was raised from the dead, we, too, shall be raised. There is great joy in that truth. That does not mean that grieving is un-Christian. The very love we have for each other honors God's creation of human beings. It mirrors the love he has for us, though a mere reflection of its complete splendor and wonder.

God shares your sorrow. He too has suffered the pain of grief when his own son was killed. He watched as Jesus cried out to him in pain. He watched as Jesus breathed his last breath. And as that Holy breath returned to heaven, God the Father received it, restored it, and raised Jesus from the grave. How magnificent a Standing Stone our Lord is! Let us go forth into the world, rejoicing in the power of the Spirit!

1. Sometimes courage is needed to go forth into the world; to face what has happened and to be determined to eventually rejoice once again. How will your courage lead you forth?

_____

_____

_____

_____

_____

_____

_____

Jamal was a bicycle courier in Manhattan. He was an ace. He could weave in and out of traffic and very rarely had to actually come to a stop, except to make a delivery. He began, "On the day the twins were attacked, I was not working my usual beat which included the Twin Towers area. I had just made a delivery and was on my way when police cars were everywhere. People were running and there were horrible noises. Screams. People yelling. I stopped in front of an electronics store," he continued, "and saw the second plane fly into the buildings. Then the towers fell."

Jamal described a sense of the surreal, that surely this could not be happening. He felt frozen and did not know what to do. He said, "For the longest time I just stood on the sidewalk, watching the footage on the televisions in the store. I can't remember any other part of that day." Jamal later finds out that his brother, a New York firefighter, was killed that day.

As soon as Ground Zero was accessible, he got on his bike and went there. He recalls the haunting sound of silence as he got closer. "St. Paul's, an Episcopal church that was next to the Towers, looked as if someone had opened a sack of flour and shaken it all over. For days there was so much dust in the air. Then all of a sudden it hit me—the dust also included the cremains of the victims. I was breathing in the people who died."

Jamal looked down at his hands. "There was a girl there on the street with a flute and she played this very sad music in the stillness of that place. It was in that split second in time I knew I had to live my life in a way that would honor the memory of those who died. I vowed to live life to the fullest every day, in boldness not fear, in honor of my brother and all those who died that day."

Angelica was a female impersonator at Pulse in Orlando. During the terrorist attack, she and some of her friends hid in the dressing room. "I could hear people screaming, some of them were my friends. I was scared I was next. The police knocked out a wall and dragged us through the air conditioning duct. When it was all over I was numb. Then I couldn't stop crying. A lot of my friends died that night. I'm not over it. I don't think I ever will be. But I have made a decision. When Pulse gets rebuilt I'm going back. I'm not a courageous person, but I am a person of faith. I know that God loves me and will be with me. I refuse to let fear control me. I'm going back in honor of all my friends who died. And I'm going to be fabulous!"

 Healing prayer for today: Precious Lord. I thank you that you not only understand my grief but are the God of compassion and mercy. Thank you for always being there—today, tomorrow, and always.

Concluding Prayers

How long does grief last? As long as it takes. But it will get easier? Yes. Just not today. As one man, who happened to be an engineer, told us, "The frequency, the intensity, and the duration begin to lessen. But I will always grieve the death of my son."

The death of a loved one can cause us to wonder if we will ever enjoy happiness again. And yet somehow if we are to honor life and to honor God in the process, we must find the courage to go on.

We are both members of the Private Grief Club. We have walked in your shoes. While everyone grieves differently we are here to tell you that we survived and so will you. While the sadness you feel will never completely go away, the consuming sorrow you feel today will begin to heal through the abundant grace of our Lord.

While it may not seem like it now, there will come a day when you will be able to transform your grief into joyful living. Maybe not today, maybe not tomorrow, but someday.

Share your story and your memories. Talk about your loved one, even if you end up having a "peep-chick moment." Tears are God's balm for healing. Think of them as holy water.

Find ways in which to honor the memory of your loved one. You are the Standing Stone that cries out that this person you loved was once alive. Their life mattered. Remembering is your legacy.

Know that we will keep you in our prayers. You are not alone. God is with you. And with his presence you will find the courage to go on. And one day you will smile again.

www.ingramcontent.com/pod-product-compliance
Lightning Source LLC
Jackson TN
JSHW081319130125
77033JS00011B/354